A LEXICON OF THE GERMAN IN
FINNEGANS WAKE

By the same author

The King Lear Perplex
Joyce's Benefictions
Two Dozen Beasts

A LEXICON OF THE GERMAN IN FINNEGANS WAKE

Helmut Bonheim

University of California Press
Berkeley and Los Angeles
1967

University of California Press
Berkeley and Los Angeles, California
© 1967 by Helmut Bonheim
Library of Congress Catalog Card Number: 65 – 21267
Printed in the Federal Republic of Germany

PREFACE

James Joyce's *Finnegans Wake* is in some senses a remarkable example of group effort: a great many people helped Joyce gather material for it over a period of seventeen years; and even a rudimentary reading of a page is best performed by a committee of scholars.

Unfortunately no scholar can be expected to come to this epic work with a knowledge of the score or so of languages which Joyce used in writing it. My list of German words in Joyce's book seeks to supply non-German readers with a modest but indispensable aid which, though dull and unconvincing by itself, when used in conjunction with *Finnegans Wake* will help penetrate the obscurities of that encyclopedic work. The reader will find that a knowledge of German adds immeasurably to his reading of the work; and it is my hope that similar lists can be prepared for the other main languages drawn upon by Joyce.

Listed are those words which are in some respect German, not in alphabetical order but according to their sequence in the book. The page and line numbers refer to American printings of 1958 and after (Viking Press) and to English editions of 1950 and after (Faber and Faber). Only in a very few instances will readers with earlier editions note minor discrepancies. For each *Wake*-word listed, the German contents of the word together with an English translation has been supplied. Some entries will seem altogether convincing in the list, less so in their context, while others may appear unlikely or farfetched in the list but useful and essential to the reader who refers back to *Finnegans Wake*. The translations are often not of the obvious dictionary sort; they are designed to convey the meaning of a German word only as it seems to be used in Joyce's text. Thus I have allowed numerous inconsistencies in citing German forms, especially verb-forms in all tenses and persons; infinitives, imperatives, or roots may be given as called for by the context. The translations are therefore unreliable for other purposes and certainly not to be recommended for students of German. Some of Joyce's German is sub-standard, non-standard, and dialect, so that North Germans will fail to recognize usages familiar to natives of Munich, Vienna, or Zurich. Indeed, the German in *Finnegans Wake* is frequently *spoken* German, as when Joyce uses "geh" instead of "gehe" with the first person pronoun (reflecting the fact that in conversation the final "e" is frequently dropped). In such cases I have not hesitated to cite the conversational (non-literary) form as the source of Joyce's usage. I have, however, made the concession to standard practice of retaining the normal German symbol for *ss* (ß) as well as the German *Umlaut*, although the digraph *(ae, oe,* or *ue)* might on occasion have usefully underlined the relationship of the *Wake*-word to its German source.

The mechanics of the list have been kept as simple as possible. The German capitalization of nouns has normally been retained, so that the reader will generally know whether an entry is a noun or a verb, but where the German source of Joyce's coinage may be verb or noun, I have usually chosen to give that form which seems most relevant in the context.

The words in the present list were included on any of a number of grounds. The least problematical entries were those which are German and nothing else—"Diener" (servant), for instance—but such pure and undebatable cases occur most rarely.

Another infrequent occurrence is the literal translation into English of a German compound. "Selfloud" looks English, but is literally *Selbstlaut* (vowel), as suggested by the context: "Where flash becomes word and silents selfloud." Permutations of this technique may be seen in a word like "innerhalf," which again looks like pure English but also echoes *innerhalb* (inside), or in an English-German coinage like "bauchspeech," in which the word *speech* is translated from *reden*, which occurs in the German *Bauchreden* (ventriloquism).

Most entries in the list are not to be explained by reference to German alone. "Shenkusmore," for instance, includes *schenk* (to give a present) and *Schenke* (a tavern or bar); but Joyce's spelling of the compound also tells us the proper pronunciation of *Senchus Mor*, the ancient Irish law, so that, were we to spell out the implications of the coinage, we would get something like "ancient laws ministering to private greed" on top of "give us another drink." Sometimes the whole coinage apes German pronunciation, but contains English elements: "Yellachters" imitates vulgar German pronunciation of *Gelächter* (laughter), on which is imposed the descriptive "yell," perhaps "yellow," and the English plural *s*.

Once we begin to appreciate the ingenuity with which Joyce creates his new language, a host of rather doubtful and arguable words present themselves for consideration. The compiler, forced to make a decision as to inclusion or rejection, must inevitably rely on his anterior explorations of Joyce's chief themes and interests as well as on his understanding of Joyce's methods of work and habits of fusing words. The context, rather than the structure of the coinage itself, must guide us to Joyce's intention. This is especially true where a knowledge of German only adds another fillip to a word which is quite explicable without that knowledge. "Flute," for instance, probably ought to remind us of the German "Flut" (flood), especially in a parody of the opening of Milton's *Paradise Lost*: "Of manifest 'tis obedience and the Flute!" We cannot be absolutely certain, but the proximate presence of Noah and the preoccupation with sin elsewhere in the book make it seem likely that the German sense of "Flute!" must be kept in mind. In the eighth chapter of Book I (the washerwomen) "main" probably refers to the German river; in the other dozen places where the word occurs, however, this meaning hardly seems relevant and there would have been no point in providing a gloss.

Many words in *Finnegans Wake* include German elements of which Joyce may well have been aware, but the explanation of which would add little to the reader's comprehension. "Bloody wars" may imply the German "war's" or "war es" to yield "Bloody was it . . ." but a knowledge of the German would not really enrich the passage for the reader. Had Joyce intended the German "war's," he could easily have suggested it by an apostrophe. If we were to examine any of a number of words on the first page of the book, such as "wielderfight," for instance, we might be induced to superimpose quantities of relatively useless interpretation on words which make sense in English: in "wielderfight" we would have to point out the *wie* (how) with which the word begins, the *er* (he) and the *der* (the), all of which would simply distract attention from the less apparent but more meaningful *wieder* (again). That Joyce intended the "wieder" we know from the "passencore rearrived" earlier in the same sentence, and from the reinforcement which the sense of *wieder* gives to one of the known themes of the book, that of cyclical repetition.[1] Therefore the *wieder* has been included in the word list, but not the probably accidental particles *wie, der,* and *er.* The inclusion of every monosyllabic German word buried in Joyce's text would have quadrupled the size of this work, swelling the list with a mass of uninteresting and irrelevant data.

The chief grounds for including any particular word, then, was its relevance to an intelligent reading of Joyce's book. The satisfaction of systematic completeness was therefore left ungratified. Some idioms, for instance, might have been explained by reference to German, but were usually left out if French or Italian seemed to explain Joyce's coinage more adequately. Generally known proper nouns such as *Fritz* and *Berlin* were usually omitted, but the understanding reader will not be offended by such entries as *Wallenstein* and *Walhalla*. Certain repeated tricks on Joyce's part could not be listed again and again, such as the *Käse* (cheese) in "Caseus," a name which occurs a great

---

[1] For this particular word we also happen to have Joyce's own gloss in a letter written late in 1929 to Miss H. S. Weaver (*Letters of James Joyce*, ed. Stuart Gilbert, New York, The Viking Press, 1957, pp. 247–248).

8

many times. The name of the hero caused similar difficulty: "Earwicker" in some of its permutations suggests *Ihr Wecker* ("your alarm clock"), a reading highly relevant to the book as a whole and to its title.

This study grew out of a search for Joyce's guiding principle in using German and perhaps other languages in his book. The fact seems to be that Joyce, who knew German extremely well (he spoke German fluently), simply used German wherever it suited him, drawing on the whole instrumentarium of the language and putting it to work as the occasion offered. He did not reserve German for, say, unsavory characters or particular situations. Where a pun offered, Joyce accepted. Already fascinated by seemingly chance connections between apparently unrelated words in English, Joyce extended his explorations of such connections into other languages. For the reader who is aware of them, these connections add to the delight occasioned by Joyce's wit and his genius for grasping poetic relevancies. The word was indeed his oyster.

ACKNOWLEDGMENTS

I am especially grateful to Fritz Senn for devoting much of his free time over a period of months to working over the first draft of this list. Since that period of cooperation over ten years ago, I have continued to enjoy his encouragement and help.

Thanks are also due to Manfred Smuda and Wolfgang Güntzel for help in checking the proofs against the 1960 Faber & Faber edition of *Finnegans Wake*, and to Herr Hans Hoffmann of Max Hueber Verlag, Munich, for helping to see a very difficult manuscript through the press.

KEY TO ABBREVIATIONS

abbrev.	abbreviation
arch.	archaic
dial.	dialect
dim.	diminutive
expl.	expletive
Gm.	German
Gm. pron.	German pronunciation
lit.	literally
MHGm.	Middle High German
pron.	pronounced
sl.	slang
sp.	spelling
vulg.	vulgar

THE LEXICON

3.6	wielderfight	wieder	again
.7	themselse	Themse	Thames
		Else	Elsa (water sprite)
.9	mishe	mische	mix
.10	tauftauf	taufen	baptize
.12	wroth, rot	rot	red
.14	regginbrow	Regen	rain
	ringsome	ringsum	all around
.15	...kamminarronn...	Kamm	comb
		Narr	fool
		(ge)ronnen	poured, flowed
.15	...tonner...	Donner	thunder
.16	...orden...	Orden	medal
4.1	gen	gen (gegen)	against
.1	gaggin	gegen	against
.5	Hoodie	Hode	testicle
.6	boomeringstroms	Strom	stream, current
.7	larms	Lärm	noise
.8	a toll, a toll	toll	mad
.14	waz iz?	was ist?	what's the matter?
.18 f	maurer	Maurer	mason
.21	sternely	Sterne	stars
.22	watsch	Watsche	slap in the face
.25	pentschanjeuchy	panschen	mix (water & wine)
.27	buildung... buildung	Bildung	education
.35	waalworth	Wahl	choice, election
5.1	himals	Himmel	sky, heaven
.2	baubletop	Bau	building, construction
.3 f	clottering	lottern	loaf
.6	Riesengeborg	Riesen	giant
		Riesengebirge	(Sudetic Mountains)
		borg-	borrow
.6	huroldry	Hure	whore
.8	fessed	Fest	holiday, festivity
		fest	solidly attached

.12	fined	Feind	enemy, fiend
.13	What then agentlike	Was denn eigentlich	What then really
.13	thundersday	Donnerstag	Thursday
.16	choruysh	Geräusch	noise
.24	bracken	brachen	broke, plowed
		Brocken	crumb
.30	wallhall's	Walhalla	(home of the gods)
		hall-	resound
.31	stonengens	eng	narrow
		Engen	narrows
.31	kisstvanes	Kiste	box
.32	tournintaxes	Thurn und Taxis	(German family, founders of postal system)
.33	basilikerks	Kerker	dungeon
.33	aeropagods	Europa	Europe
.35	mecklenburk	meck	(goat's cry)
		Mecklenburg	(territory on the Baltic Sea)
6.5	thurum . . . thurum	Turm	tower
.6	uproor	Aufruhr	commotion, revolt
.6	aufroofs . . . roof	Aufruf	summons, appeal
		Ruf	call
.7	reef	rief	called
.9 f	stottered	stottern	stutter
.18	raiders	Räder	wheels
.22	Belling	bellen	to bark
.24	bier	Bier	beer
.25	sich	sich	himself
.25	deepbrow	Dieb	thief
		Brau	brew
.26	bockalips	Bock	goat, bock beer
.27	hoer	hör-	listen, hear
.30	tautaulogically	Tau	dew, hawser
.35 f	a horn	Ahorn	maple
7.3	flittaflute	Flut	flood
.4	issavan essavans	iß, eß-	eat
.5	toll	toll	mad
.6	Taubling	taub	deaf
		Taube	dove

.7	gross	groß	large
.8	So sigh us	so sei es	so be it
		Sozius	companion
.9	sprids	spritz	spray
.13	fraudstuff	Frau	wife, woman
.15	yestern	gestern	yesterday
		Stern	star
.17	woebecanned	wohlbekannt	well known
.17	packt	packt	packs, grabs
18	schlook	schluck-	swallow
		schlug	beat
.18	schlice	Schleiß	splinter
.31	starck	stark	strong
.31	mund	Mund	mouth
.35 f	hockums	hocken	squat
8.1	Wallinstone	Wallenstein	(general)
.25	argaumunt	Aargau	(Swiss canton)
		Gaum-	gums
		Mund	mouth
.31	legahorns	Ahorn	maple
.34	band	Bande	gang
.35	mormorial	Marmor	marble
.35	obscides	abseits	aside
.36	hrosspower	Roß	steed
9.4	Yaw, yaw, yaw	ja	yes
.5	Leaper	lieber	dear
.5	Fear siecken	Vier	four
		wir siegen	we conquer
		siechen	waste away
.5	Fieldgaze thy tiny frow	Wie geht's deiner Frau?	How's your wife?
.11 f	hurold	Hure	whore
.20	Futter	Futter	fodder
.26	Almeidagad	Alm	alp
		meid-	avoid
		Eid	oath
.26 f	Brum! Brum!	brumm-	grumble, rumble
.27	Underwetter	Donnerwetter	thunderweather (expletive)
		Unwetter	storm

.27 f	Goat strip Finnlambs	Gott strafe England	may God punish England (WW I slogan)
.28	rinning	rinnen	run, flow
.28 f	ousterlists	Auster	oyster
		List	deception
.32	bissmark	Biß	bite
		Mark	(money)
.34	marmorial	Marmor	marble
.36	fimmieras	für immer	for ever
10.5	lipsyg	Leipzig	(city)
.5	krieging	Krieg	war
		krieg-	get
.5	funk	Funk	spark, radio
.7	wixy	Wichse	shoeblacking, thrashing
.9	bombshoob	Schub	push
.25	keling	Kehle	throat
.28 f	nummered	Nummer	number
.34	helfalittle	helf-	help
		elf	eleven
.35	wrothschields	rot	red
		Schild	sign
		schiel-	leer, squint
.35	Lumproar	Lump	scoundrel
11.3	on shower	Anschauer	observer
.4	Nixy	Nixe	water nymph
.5	Neblas	Nebel	fog
.9	peacefugle	Vogel	bird
.11	bickybacky	Bickbeere	bilberry
		Backe	cheek
.13	plunderpussy	Plunder	trash, rubbish
.16	nebo	neben	next to
.26	bucklied	Lied	song
.29	bootifull	Boot	boat
.29 f	strengly forebidden	streng	stern
		verboten	forbidden
.35	saack	sag-	say
12.2	citters	zitter-	tremble
.4	butteler's	Bettler	beggar

.8	floote	Flut	flood
.8 f	glaubrous	glaub-	believe
.9	Herrschuft	Herr	mister, gentleman
		Schuft	scoundrel
		Herrschaft	mastery
.9	Whatarwelter	Wetter	weather
		Welt	world
.11	puff	Puff	thump, brothel (sl.)
.17	hin	hin	thence, gone
.20	himples	Himmel	sky, heaven
.21	heegills	Hügel	hill
.23	taffetaffe	tauf-	baptize
		Affe	ape
.23	Wharton's	warten	wait, waiting
.26	bergins	Berge	mountains
		bergen	recover, conceal
.27	bergamoors	Berg	mountain
.27	bergagambols	Berg	mountain
.28	bergincellies	Berge	mountains
		bergen	recover, conceal
.29	bergones	Berg	mountain
.35	macroborg	borg-	borrow
.36	microbirg	birg	recover, conceal
13.18	forover	vorüber	past
.23	fear	vier	four
.32	fassilwise	Faß	cask
.32	pass how	Passau	(Bavarian town on Danube)
.33	wondern	wandern	wander
.34	Whallfisk	Walfisch	whale
14.2	sothisfeige	Feige	fig, vagina
		feige	cowardly
.7	brazenlockt	lockt	allures, beckons
.8	Puppette	Puppe	doll
.12	Primas	Prima	(school grade)
		prima	first class
		Primas	archbishop
.31	fredeland's	Fried-	peace
		Friedel	dim. of Gottfried
		edel	noble

.32	crook	Krücke	crutch
15.4	rings round	rings 'rum	all around
.5	perihelygangs	Gang	walk, gait
.14	norgels	nörgeln	complain
		Orgel	organ
.15	surssurhummed	surr-	hum
.17	duncledames	dunkel	dark
.17	hellish	hell	bright
.36	alebrill	Brille	spectacles
16.1 f	michindaddy	mich	me
.11	pleasurad	Rad	wheel
.16	mutter	Mutter	mother
.17	stummer	Stummer	mute person
.18	hauhauhauhaudibble	hau-	hit, thrash
.24	a bitskin	a' bißchen	a little
.29	eyegonblack	eigen	own
		Augenblick	moment
.30	qualm	Qualm	thick smoke
.30	trink gilt	Trinkgeld	tip
		gilt	is worth, counts
17.6	brookcells	Bruck- (dial.)	bridge
.9	Rooks	Ruck	jolt
.10	roome	Ruhm	fame
.10	snore	schnore	(Swiss:) talk, chatter
.13	when	wenn	if
.14	forsstand	verstand	understood, reason
		Vorstand	chairman
.15	rutterdamrotter	Götterdämmerung	twilight of the gods
.15 f	umscene	umsehen	look around
.16	Gut	gut	good
.19	Elters	Eltern	parents
.19	wone	wohn-	reside
		Wonne	delight
.23	Punct	Punkt	period, full stop
.23	ruhmuhrmuhr	ruh-	rest
		Ruhm	fame
		Uhr	clock
.25	craching	Krach	crash, quarrel
.27	netherfallen	niederfallen	fall down

.27	plage	Plage	plague
.27	flick	flick-	patch, mend
		flink	quick
.30	erde from erde	Erde	earth
.32	Hereinunder	herein	in, come in
		hinunter	downward
.34 f	alp ... drukn	Alp	mountain
		drucken	print
		drücken	press
		Alpdruck	nightmare
.36	iz leebez	ist Liebes	is love's
18.1	'Zmorde	Mord	murder
.2	Meldundleize	melden	to announce
		mild und leise	mild and soft
			(Wagner's
			Tristan)
.2	behoughted	behauptet	asserted
.3	thanacestross	Roß	steed
.5	roturns	rot	red
.6	rede	Rede	speech
.9	whisht	wischt	wipes
.13	graab	Grab	grave
.18	rede	rede-	speak
.20	Tieckle	Tieck	Ludwig Tieck
			(romantic
			novelist)
.22	meandertale	Tal	valley
		Neanderthal	(German valley
			where stone age
			skeletons found)
.23	Heidenburgh	Heiden	heathen
		Burg	fortress
		Heidelberg	(city)
.29 f	vivelyonview	(lit.) Lebens-	philosophy of life
		anschauung	
.30	-onview	(lit.) Anblick	scene, sight
.35	firefing	fing	caught
.35	flintforfall	Vorfall	incident
19.5	rangled	rang	wrestled

.8 f	kimmells	Kümmel	caraway
		Kimm	bilge
.11	oldwolldy	Wolle	wool
		woll-	wish
.25	meanderthalltale	Tal	valley
		hall-	resound
		Neanderthal	(German valley)
.30	ahnsire	Ahn	ancestor
		ahn-	suspect
.31	papeer	Papier	paper
.33	boot	Boot	boat
20.1 f	milchcamel	Milch	milk
.7	muttheringpot	Mutter	mother
		Hering	herring
.7	Gutenmorg	guten Morgen	good morning
.8	tintingfast	Tintenfaß	inkwell
		fast	almost
.12	endlike	endlich	finally
.17	sunder	Sünder	sinner
.20	kindlelight	Kindl	child
		kindeln	to trifle
.25	strubbely	struppig	shaggy, rough
.30	gelding	Geld	money
.31	mischievmiss	misch-	mix
.33	trippiery	Tripper	gonorrhea
.34	expectungpelick	-ung	(German suffix of quality or condition)
.35	besch	Esche	ash tree
.36	Hohore	höre	listen
21.2	wis	wiß-	know
.5	lang	lang	long
.18	Wans	Wanze	bug
		Wanst	belly
.19	skirtmissches	misch-	mix
.20	handworded	antwortet	answers
.23	deef	Dieb	thief
.29	tauch	tauch-	dive
.30	luderman	Luder	bait, lure scoundrel

22.2	wringing	ringen	wrestle
.2	brodar	Bruder	brother
.3 f	flackering	flackern	flare, flicker
.4	witter	witter-	perceive, scent
		Wetter	weather
		Gewitter	storm
.6	handwording	antworten	answer
.9	atter	Attersee	(Austrian lake)
.18	be dom ter	Dom	cathedral
		verdammter	damned
.30	skirtmishes	misch-	mix
.35	hemmed	Hemd	shirt
23.6	... kur ... barg ...	Kur	cure
	mitghund ...	barg	carried, revealed
		mit	with
		Hund	dog
.7	... mull ...	Müll	garbage
.9	shurts	Schürze	apron
.10	kirssy	Kirsche	cherry
.14	hearsomeness	gehorsam	obedient
.15	burger	Bürger	citizen
.20	festyknees	feste	solid, sturdy
.21	Wolkencap	Wolken	clouds, cloud-
.25	Hairfluke	Herr	Mr., gentleman
		verflucht	accursed, damn (expl.)
.25	Impalpabunt	bunt	colorful
.26	abhears	ab	off
		abhören	wiretap, hear recitation
.32	loab	Lob	praise
		Leib	body
		Laib	loaf
.32	hold	hold	handsome
.33	pudor puff	Puder	powder
		Puff	brothel
.33	libe	Leib	body
.35	spier	Spier	thin stalk
24.1	Nilbud	Nil	Nile

.12	youngers	Junge	boy
		Jünger	disciple
.14	*Usqueadbaugham*	Baum	tree
.21	Bower	Bauer	farmer
25.21	to free	freien	woo
.25	buddhoch	hoch	high, hurrah
.27	Erinnes	erinner-	remember
		Rinne	gutter, groove
.28	Brettland	Brett	board
.32	reise	Reise	journey
26.17	unrested	unruhig	disturbed
.18	Totumcalmum	tot	dead
27.6	knicks	Knicks	curtsy
.8	ide	Eid	oath
.8	laus	Laus	louse
.9	knirps	Knirps	mannikin
.14	Essie	es	it
		sie	she
.24 f	spooring	spüren	to sense
.28	angst	Angst	fear
.29	misches	misch-	mix
.29	kind	Kind	child
.35	stump entirely	Stumpen	cheap cigar
.36	sternwheel's	Stern	star
28.5	salig	selig	happy, delighted
.11	guldenselver	Gulden	guilder, florin
.13	ribbons	Rippen	ribs
.24	Ding	Ding	thing
.30	flattering	flatter-	waver
.31	Worther	Wörter	words
29.2	buaboabaybohm	Buab (dial.)	boy
.4	ivoeh!	I wo!	(expletive of astonishment, disbelief)
.4	showm	Schaum	foam
.6	senken	senken	submerge, lower
.8	twilling	Zwilling	twin
.32	honnein	nein	no
30.1 f	O'Rangans	Gans	goose
.7	Ankers	Anker	anchor

.9	wapentake	Wappen	coat-of-arms
.11	Hofed-	Hof	court
31.10	thon	Ton	sound; clay
.12	gift	Gift	poison
.28	kinned	kennt	knows
.32	allegibelling	alle	everyone
		bell-	bark (verb)
32.3	for seeks	versuch-	try
.27	oxgangs	Gang	gait, walk
.29	Wallenstein	Wallenstein	(Austrian general)
.29	Semperkelly's	Kelle	trowel
.29	immergreen	immer	always, ever
33.24	Kellikek	Kelle	trowel
		keck	bold, impudent
.27	Hoq, hoq, hoq!	Hoch!	hurray!
.34	pfuit! pfuit!	pfui!	shame!
.36	abhout	haut ab	decamps
34.3	Gamellaxarksky	Gamelle	food basin
.33	malers	Maler	painter
35.9	hideinsacks	Heiden	heathen
		dein	yours
		ein	one, in
.9	blaufunx	Blaufuchs	blue fox
		blau	blue
		Funk-	spark
.13	schulder	Schuld	guilt
		Schulter	shoulder
.14	coumfry	kaum frei	hardly free
.31	ton	Ton	tone
.32	toller	toll	mad
36.5	Morganspost	Morgen	morning, tomorrow
		Gans	goose
.10 f	toosammenstucked	zusammen	together
.14	drumdrum	drum	therefore
.16	hough	Hauch	breath
		hoch	high
.16	ellboge	Ellbogen	elbow
.30	withdwellers	Mitwohner	p. sharing living quarters
.35	stern	Stern	star

.36	it was to make	es war zu machen	it had to be done
			it could be done
37.1	mannleich	männlich	masculine
		Mann	man
		Leiche	corpse
.2	lufted	Luft	air
.5	guilders	Gelder	funds
.6	abock	Bock	goat
.14	tag	Tag	day
.15	verbaten	verboten	forbidden
.20	flitmansfluh	Fluh	precipice
.21	mude unswer	müde	tired
		uns	us
		schwer	hard
.23	in the blowne	im Blauen	in the blue
.29	*spuckertuck*	spuck	spit
		spuken	haunting
		Tuch	cloth
.32	pilzenpie	Pilz	mushroom
.33	senaffed	Affe	ape
.34	balled	bald	soon
.34 f	proviant	Proviant	provision
38.9	Maxwelton	Welten	worlds
.11 f	Pomeranzia	Pomeranze	pomegranate
		ranzig	rancid
.13	curtsey	Kürze	brevity
.29	ruah	Ruhe	quiet
.33	my bravor	mein Braver	my good one
.33	fraur	Frau	wife, woman
39.14	wetter	Wetter	weather
.14	renns	renn-	race
.35	herbage	Herberge	hostelry
40.2	leababobed	lieb	dear
		Liebe	love
.17	Mildew Lisa	mild und leise	gentle and soft
.22	rootie	Rute	switch, twig
.23	selfabyss	Biß	bite
.25	natigal's	Nachtigall	nightingale
41.13	bakenbeggfuss	Fuß	foot
.14	shinkhams	Schinken	ham

.19	puncta	Punkt	period
.20	habenny	haben	have
.20 f	oberflake	ober	over
		Oberfläche	surface
42.11	seinn	sein	to be
.12	seinn	sein	to be
.14	cumannity	Kummer	sorrow
		Mann	man
.15	bogeyer	Geier	vulture
		Eier	eggs
.17	lieder	Lieder	songs
.27	Hardmuth's	Mut	courage
43.2	hamalags	Hammel	mutton
.8	tassing	Tasse	cup
.23	*Artahut*	Art	kind
		Hut	hat
.36	sputabout	sput-	hurry
44.7	rann	rann	flowed
.9	viersified	vier	four
.11	Lug	Lug	lie
		(Swiss for Lüge)	
.13	Soll	soll	should
.13	will	will	wants
.19	brumming	brummen	buzz, grunt, snarl
.20	. . . klatschab . . .	Klatsch	applaud, gossip
		schab	scrape
.21	. . . grad . . .	Grad	degree
.21	. . . kot!	Kot	dirt, excrement
46.4	Bargainweg	gehen weg	go away
		Weg	way
47.15	frew	Fru (dial. for Frau)	wife, woman
48.10	Inkermann	Eckermann	(writer)
.12	Austelle	ausstellen	make out, issue
		Stelle	place
.19	Osti-Fosti	Ost	East
49.4	Zassnoch!	das noch!	that too!
.6	alohned	Lohn	reward
.34	Micholas	mich	me
50.2	uns	uns	us
.5	candlestock	Stock	stick

.10	austral	Auster	oyster
.11	spoorlessly	Spur	track
		spurlos	without a trace
.17	funster's	Fenster	window
.17	finsterest	finster	dark
.19	treu	treu	loyal
.19	troster	Trost	solace
.30 f	yearschaums	Schaum	foam
		Meerschaum	Meerschaum
.36	nebuless	Nebel	fog
51.4	scherzarade	Scherz	joke
.7	lavaleer	leer	empty
.14	haardly	Haar	hair
.15	Enkelchums	Enkel	grandchild
.16	jongers	Jünger	disciple
		Junge	boy
.17	nine!	nein	no
.30	inselt	Insel	island
.34	duldrum	duld-	suffer
.36	fragrend	frag-	ask
52.9	Tolkaheim	Heim	home
.16	fraulino	Frau	wife, woman
		Fräulein	miss
.20	burst	bürst-	brush
.25	Toll	toll	mad
.27	finndrinn	drin	within
.27	knopfs	Knopf	button
.35	sukand see whybe!	suchen Sie (das)	search for the
		Weib	woman
53.4	oedor	oede (öde)	waste, desertlike
.13	eren	Ehren	honors
.16	stark	stark	strong
.18	belling	bell-	bark
.18 f	doerehmoose	Reh	deer
.23	soide	Seide	silk
.24	manfally	Falle	trap
.24	lekan	lecken	lick
.27	gothsprogue	Sprache	language
.31	Tomach's	mach's	do it
.34	hoch	hoch	high

.35	hitz	Hitze	heat
54.1	Hup	hup-	honk
.5	Vogt	Vogt	overseer, warden, constable
.7	list	List	stealth
.18	Wee fee?	wieviel?	how much?
.24	sicker	sicher	surely
.25	househalters	Haushälter	householder
.25	yorehunderts	Jahrhundert	century
.27	guesthouse	Gasthaus	inn
.27	cowhaendel	Handel	trade
		Kuhhandel	shady business
.30	forthstretched	(lit.:) ausstrecken	extend, reach out
.33 f	mutsohito	Mut	courage
55.1	lobe	Lob	praise
.4	mundibanks	Mund	mouth
.13	huts	Hut	hat
.15	homd	Hemd	shirt
.15	dicky	Dicke	fat person
.16	peajagd	Jagd	hunt
.23	rundreisers	rund	around
		Reise	travel
		Rundreise	tour
.24	beheld	Held	hero
.26	frore ... frore	fror	froze
.30	asches	Asche	ash
.30	peins	Pein	pain, torture
56.7	Reef	rief	called
.7	whallrhosmightiadd	Walroß	walrus
		Roß	steed
.14	stod tillsteyne	stillstehen	stand still
		Stein	stone
.14	meisies	Meise	titmouse
		Ameise	ant
.15	rung	gerungen	wrestled
.19	akkurat	Kur	cure; election
		Rat	advice
.25	stockfisch	Stockfisch	stockfish
.26	herberged	Herberge	shelter, inn
.34	Tal	Tal	valley

.35	grube	Grube	hole, mine, scar
.35	orfishfellows'	orphisch	orphic
.36	regnans	regnen	rain
57.4	folkers	Völker	peoples
.7	hantitat	Tat	deed
.11	alplapping	plappern	gossip
.12	coyly coiled um	Keule	club
		um	around
.14	Jotnursfjaell	Jot	letter j
		nur	only
		ja	yes
		Fell	skin
.14	grummelung	Grummel	distant thunder
.18	irreperible	irre	mad, mistaken
.27	maugdleness	mau	middling
		Magd	maid
		Auge	eye
.27	mild dewed	milde	mild
.30	Eher	eher	rather
		ehern	brazen
57.32	outlander	Ausländer	foreigner
58.9	schreis	Schrei	shriek
.12	Flucher's	Flucher	one who curses
.13	fettle	Vettel	slut
.13	wohl	wohl	well
.17 f	seufsighed	seufzen	sigh
.18	for gassies	vergiß es	forget it
.18	threnning	Trennung	separation
.19	kuo	Kuo (Swiss and old high German for Kuh)	cow
.23 f	Refuseleers	Fusel	gin
		leer	empty
.24	Peingpeong	Pein	pain, suffering
.31	stilstand	Stil	style
		Stillstand	halt, armistice
59.7	lallance	lallen	babble
.9	hollegs	Hölle	hell
.11	sprangflowers	sprang	exploded

.12	reinworms	rein	pure
		Regenwurm	earthworm
.17	Achburn	ach!	oh!
.25	hosing	Hosen	trousers
.26	hosed	Hose	trousers
.29	Eiskaffier	Eiskaffee	iced coffee
.31	Good, mein leber!	Leber	liver
		mein lieber Gott!	dear God!
.32	umbedimbt!	um	around
		unbedingt	certainly
60.10	Benkletter	kletter-	climb
.26	brut . . . brut	Brut	brood
.32	probiverbal	Probe	attempt, rehearsal
61.4	bachelure's	Bach	brook
62.3	baggermalster	Bürgermeister	mayor
.8	bilder	Bilder	pictures
.10	mine	mein	my
.10	giftake	Gift	poison
.10	hosenband	Hosenband	belt
		Hosenbandorden	order of the garter
.11	halter	halt	hold, stop
63.6	gaeilish	Eile	hurry
		geil	insolent, lewd
.27	fillthefluthered	Flut	flood
.33	stoub	Staub	dust
64.2	obi ohny	ob	whether
		ohne	without
.13 f	musikants'	Musikant	musician
.16	reine	Reine	the pure one
.18	schurts	Schurz, Schürze	apron
.19	wischandtugs	wischen	wipe
		Handtuch	towel
.20	wasching	wasch-	wash
.20	walters	walt-	manage, govern
.20	weltering walters	Welt	world
		Wetter	weather
		walt-	govern
.31	berbecked	Ecke	corner
		Beck (dial.)	baker
.31	fischial	Fisch	fish

.32	machelar's	mach-	make, do
.36	Elders	Eltern	parents
65.4	Leer	leer	empty
.5	geeser	Gießer	p. who pours, sprinkles
.17	tolloll	toll	mad
.31	tofftoff	tauf-	baptize
.32	Farber	Farbe	color
.34	Ack, ack, ack	ach	oh
.36	so to singen	singen	sing
		sozusagen	so to speak
66.4	nachtistag	Nacht	night
		Tag	day
		Nachtigall	nightingale
.13	hucks	huck-	squat
.13	gummibacks	Gummi	rubber
.17	afterwite	After	anus
.18	lappish	läppisch	silly, childish
.23	Hahn	Hahn	rooster
.25	kiribis	Kürbis	pumpkin
.32	Oetzmann	Mann	man
67.2	mid their nackt	Mitternacht	midnight
		nackt	naked
.10	heiterscene	heiter	merry
.11	Tobkids	tob-	rage, play violently
.15	querrshnorrt	quer	across
		schnorren	cadge
68.6	*huck*	hucken	squat
.15	valkirry	Walküre	Valkyrie
		kirre	tame, allure
.19	Bissavolo	biß	bite
.21	Tawfulsdreck!	Teufelsdreck	devil's dung
.21	reine	Reine	pure one
.31	erpressgangs	erpress-	blackmail, extort
		Gang	walk, gait
.35	yeeklings	Klinge	blade, sword
		kling-	ring, chime
69.9	orts and oriorts	Ort	place, village
.10	garthen	Garten	garden
.11	Armen	Armen	poor people

.25	triplepatlockt	lockt	beckons
.32	Herr Betreffender	Herr	Mr.
		Betreffender	with reference to, the one concerned
.32	zimmer	Zimmer	room; (author)
.35 f	Kommerzial	Kommerzial(rat)	commercial (councillor)
.36	Zentral	Zentral	central
70.1	Osterich	Österreich	Austria
.1	Gaul	Gaul	horse, nag
.3	Yuly wheil	Juli	July
		weil	because
		heil	hail; healthy
.4	swobbing	Schwaben	Swabia
.4	brockendootsch	Brocken	morsel, crumb
		deutsch	German
.5	Der Fall Adams	der Fall Adams	the case of Adam
.5	Siding	Zeitung	newspaper
.6	Fastland	fast Land	almost land
		Festland	continent
.6	er, consstated	er	he
		konstatier-	aver
.7	lammswolle	Lammswolle	lamb's wool
.7	and wider	und weiter	and further
.8	same	Samen	seed
.8	zurichschicken	zurückschicken	send back
.8 f	tosend and obertosend	tausend und abertausend	thousands and thousands
		tosen	roar, rage
		ober	over
.9	tonnowatters	Donnerwetter	thunder weather (expletive)
		Watte	cotton wool
.16	bierd	Bier	beer
.17	deposend	Posen	(city)
.17	bockstump	Bock	goat
.21	hirsuiter	Hirse	millet
71.8 f	Inkermann	Eckermann (Crimean Inkerman has one n)	(author)

.17	Blau Clay	blau- Klee	blue clover
.18	Gobblasst	blaß	pale
		laßt	leave
		Last	burden
.20	Mundzucker	Mund	mouth
		Zucker	sugar
.33	Clandorf	Dorf	village
.34	Arschmann	Arschmann	assman
72.2	Twitchbratschballs	Bratsche	viola
.3	Burgaans	Burg	fortress
		Gans	goose
.12	Bad	Bad	bath
.12	Humborg	Hamburg	(city)
		borg-	borrow
.13	Hraabhraab	Rabe	raven
.13	Coocoohandler	Kuhhandel	shady deal
.13	Miching	mich	me
.23	fuchsiar	Fuchs	fox
.25	ihm, Gonn	ihm	him
		gönn-	grant, permit
.27	glatt	glatt	smooth
.35 f	splish the splume	Plisch [und] Plum	(W. Busch story)
73.2	Hyland	Heiland	Savior
.15	Elf	elf	eleven
.17	solgier	Gier	greed
.21	lurch	Lurch	batrachian
.21	Bach	Bach	(composer), brook
.24	siegings	siegen	triumph (verb), win
		sie ging	she went
.26	-an-	an	to
.26	Bangen-	bangen	be afraid
74.9	faustive	Faust	fist
.14	nassy	naß	wet
.14	adrone	drohen	threaten
.17	Rethfernhim	fern	distant
75.1	teargarten	Tiergarten	zoo
.3	Marmarazalles	Marmor	marble
.3	Marmeniere	Niere	kidney
.4	sigilposted	Siegel	seal

.5	stil	Stil	style
		still	quietly
.11	habben to upseek	haben aufzusuchen	have to look up
.17	gift	Gift	poison
.17	saft eyballds	Saft	juice
		Ei	egg
		bald	soon
.19	engles	Engel	angel
.21	rab	Rabe	raven
76.4	guestfriendly	(lit.) gastfreundlich	hospitable
.8	sicker	sicher	surely
.8	taal	Tal	valley
.13	liever	Lieber	dear one
.17	koorts	kurz	short
.20	neuw	neu	new
.20	klerds	Erd-	earth
.23	Wacht	Wacht	guard; awake
.26	troutbeck	Becken	basin, pool
.32	erst	erst	first
.32	treubleu	treu	loyal
		blau	blue
.32	Donawhu	Donau	Danube
.36	architecht	echt	genuine
77.3	misterbilder	Mist	garbage
		Bilder	pictures
.6	sternbooard	Stern	star
.13	Oorlog	Uhr	clock
		Ohr	ear
.14	vogt	Vogt	bailiff, warden
.14	pfife	Pfeife	pipe
.14 f	whaanever	Wahn	false opinion, delusion
.15	blaetther	Blätter	leaves
.18	fassed	fast	almost
		Faß	keg
.20	insteppen	eintreten	enter
.20 f	alls als hats	als hätt's	as though it had
.21 f	hoofd offdealings	Hof	court
		(lit.) Abteilungen	compartments, departments

.22	ladykants te huur	Kante	edge
		könnt's d'Uhr	could you (tell me) the time?
		Hure	whore
.27	gohellt	gehellt	illuminated
.27	Heer Herewhippit	Heer	army
		Herr	Mr.
.29	blasses	blaß	pale
.30	Hoodendoses	Hoden	testicles
		Dose	box, canister
.30	reekwaterbeckers	Riechwasser	perfume
		Becher	beaker
		Becken	basin
.31	zootzaks	Zoten	obscenities
.31	eatlust	(lit.) Eßlust	appetite
.32	rookworst	Rauchwurst	smoked sausage
		rückwärts	backwards
.34	met	mit	with
.36	wandelingswight	Wandel	behavior, change
		Wandlung	transformation
78.5	Donnaurwatteur!	Donnerwetter	thunderweather (expletive)
		Donau	Danube
		Watte	cotton wool
.5	Hunderthunder!	Hundert	hundred
		Hunde	dogs
.5	grosskopp	groß	large
		Kopf	head
.7	Zeit's	Zeit	time
.7	Blueblitzbolted	Blitz	lightning
.8	hingeworms	(lit.) Angelwurm	angling-worm
.9	Gehinnon	geh	go
		hinnen	from hence
.10	Unterwealth	Unterwelt	underworld
.12	propaguting	gut	good
.16	Foughtarundser	Vater Unser	Our Father
		rund	round
.19	monads	Monat	month
.20	aardappel	Erdapfel	potato

.21	dreyfussed	drei	three
		Fuß	foot
.23	patrizien	Patrizier	patrician
.27	bluemin	Blumen	flowers
79.5	Ewacka	wacker	brave
.18	vulcans	Vulkan	volcano
.29	elvanstone	Elfenbein	ivory
.30	stinkend	stinkend	stinking
.35	gulden	Gulden	(coin)
80.7	tautaubapptossed	tauf-	baptize
		Tau	dew
		taub	deaf
.14	leabhar	lieber	dear one
		Haar	hair
.18	Give over	(lit.) übergeben	deliver; vomit; give up
.20	sprack	Sprache	language
.24	araflammed	Flamme	flame
.26	goharksome	gehorsam	obedient
81.6	faultering	faul	lazy
.7	tramestrack	Strecke	tracks, line
	by Brahm	Brahm	(stage manager, critic)
.11	Halte!	halte	stop
.13	buchan	Buch	book
		Buchen	beech-trees
.14	Lautrill	Laut	loud; sound
.14	Brennan's	brennen	burn
.16	traums	Traum	dream
.28	patrecknocksters	Ecke	corner
.31	holst	Holst	holly
.35	man	man	one
82.3	tipperuhry	Ruhr	(district); diarrhea
		rühr-	stir; affect emotions
		Ruh	rest
.4	toller	toller	(author); wilder, madder

.21 f	not his shirt to tear, to know wanted, joking and knob-kerries all aside laying	(German word order)	
.28	Yuni or Yuly	Juni	June
		Juli	July
.30	mauled	Maul	mouth, muzzle
		maul-	mope, sulk
.36	Yuddanfest	Judenfest	Jewish holiday
83.3	baches	Bach	(composer); brook
.10	Nichtian	nicht	not
.13	sprogues	Sprache	language
.17	pearlmothers	Perlmutter	mother of pearl
.29	faust	Faust	fist
.35 f	schmallkalled	schmal	narrow
	the treatyng	Schmalkaldischer Bund	Treaty of Schmalkalden
84.5	rhumanasant	Ruhm	fame
.10	wunder	Wunder	wonder
.16 f	deinderivative	dein	your
.27	Herwho	Herr	Mr.
.30	wurming	Wurm	worm
.34	politish	politisch	political
85.5	hole	hole	fetch
.9	thrufahrts	Durchfahrt	thoroughfare, passage
.11	alpenstuck	Alpenstock	alpenstock
		Stuck	plaster
.16	naturlikevice	natürlich	natural
.25	plomansch	Mansch	mixture, squash
.31	Oyeh! Oyeh!	Oje!	oh dear!
86.1	sparse	spar-	save
.3	quatz	Quatsch	nonsense
.4 f	to stick fire	(lit.) Feuer anzustecken	to light a fire
.5	feacht	Acht	care, attention
.7	Robort	Abort	privy
		Ort	place

.12	feishts	feist	fat
.13	Rabworc	Rabe	raven
.26	doorweg	Weg	way
		weg	away
.34	Nullnull	null null, 00	zero zero, sign for toilet
87.8	Yetstoslay	jetzt	now
.16	friedhoffer	Friedhof	cemetery
		Fried-	peace
		hoff-	hope
.22	polarbeeber	Biber	beaver
.32	O'Donner	Donner	thunder
88.2	abfalltree	Abfall	garbage; apostasy
		Apfel	apple
.5	basel to boot	Baselbut	region around Basel
.12	lugs	Lüge	lie
.18	nase	Nase	nose
.19	aastalled	Aas	carrion
.23	Yggdrasselmann	Mann	man
.26	rock	Rock	coat, skirt
.30	aleland	Elend	misery
.33	Portterand's	Rand	border, edge
.33	Wirrgeling	wirr	confused
		würgen	choke
		geling	succeed
89.7	Rooskayman	Ruß	soot
	kamerad	Kamerad	comrade
.9	smuked	Schmuck	jewelry, decoration
.12	yellowatty	Watte	cotton wool
.28	vulcano	Vulkan	volcano
.33	Arm	arm	poor
.33	ethnic fort	nicht fort	not gone
.35	ture	Türe	door
.36	bit to	bitte	please
90.2	buxers	Büchse	box
.3	Tob	tob-	rage, rave
.8 f	morkernwindup	Kern	kernel
.11	shrecks	Schreck	fright
.11	neckanicholas'	necken	tease
.17	fort	fort	gone

.18	jah	ja	yes
.24	bruck	Brücke	bridge
.28	ach	ach	oh
.28	Oo	OO	sign for toilet
.28	Augs	Auge	eye
.28	ohrs	Ohr	ear
.28 f	O'kehley	Kehle	throat
.31 f	... moecklenburg ...	Mecklenburg	(territory on the Baltic Sea)
.32	... tastrump ...	tast-	touch
.33	... nach	nach	after
.34	Meirdreach	ach	ah
91.11	gutthroat	gut	good
.28	iskybaush	Bausch	bunch, compress (noun)
.28 f	abgod	Abgott	idol
.30	Warhorror	Walhalla	(home of the gods)
92.2 f	yellachters	Gelächter	laughter
.8	onesame	einsam	lonely, single
.9	himundher	hin und her	hither and thither
		Mund	mouth
		und	and
.13	Show'm	Schaum	foam
.17	O feen	fein	excellent
.24	defeme	Feme	vehmic court
93.13	krigkry	Krieg	war
		krieg-	get
.15	gratiasagam	sag-	say
.16	biss	biss	bit
.24	bitther	bitte	please
.36	strenghth	streng	stern
94.1	gretnass	Gräte	fishbone
		nass	wet
.2	Meldon	melden	announce
.8	uptied	(lit.) aufgebunden	untied
.10	perlection	Perle	pearl
.14	threne	Träne	tear
.14	furchte fruchte	fürchte Früchte	fear fruits
.15	frai	frei	free
.15	frau	Frau	woman

.16	ana mala	einmal	once
.16	amygdaleine	Magd	maid
		Mägdelein	little maid
		Leine	leash
.17	obster	ob	whether
		Obst	fruit
.18	fromm	fromm	pious
.28	dring	dring-	press, penetrate
.30	beetyrossy	bitte	please
		Beete	flower beds
		Roß	steed
.36	preester	Priester	priest
95.2 f	Ballybock	Bock	he-goat
.4	rossies chaffing	Roß	steed
		schaffen	create, provide
.22	kissabetts	Bett	bed
.28	anschluss	Anschluß	connection
.30	fern	fern	distant
.33	hast	hast	(you) have
.34	craigs	Krieg	war
96.24	schenkusmore	schenk uns mehr	pour us more, give us more
.31	stotter	stotter-	stutter
97.2	outratted	(lit.) ausrotten	exterminate
.5	Lœwensteil	Löwenanteil	lion's share
		steil	steep
		Stiel	stick, handle
.10	Boolies	Buhle	lover
.13 f	fuchser's	Fuchs	fox
.19	whilk	welche?	which?
		welk	withered
.20	spasoakers	Spaß	joke, fun
.21	protown	(lit.) Vorort	suburb
.27	winceywency	winzig	tiny
.30	libber	lieber	dear
.36	epheus	Efeu	ivy
98.1	wimmering	wimmer-	whimper
.1	weibes	Weib	woman, wife
.2	bang	bang	apprehensive

.3	noase	Nase	nose
		As	ace; A flat (music)
.3 f	blem, blem	blem	crazy
.5	-shema	Schema	scheme
.6	ankered	Anker	anchor
		kehr-	sweep
.24	demifrish	frisch	fresh
.26	fas	Faß	barrel
		faß-	grab
.27	auchnomes	auch	also
.28	gar ganz	gar	even; cooked
		ganz	all
		Gans	goose
.30	Heer	Heer	army
		Herr	gentleman, Mr.
.32	wiege	Wiege	cradle
.32	wiege ne'er a waage	Wiege	cradle
		Waage	scale
		wage	dare

Ref. to joke that man says to young lady „Wenn ich eine Wiege hätte, würde ich etwas wagen" (If I had a cradle I'd dare something) instead of „Wenn ich eine Waage hätte, würde ich etwas wiegen" (If I had a scale I'd weigh something).

.32 f	still immer and	still	quiet
	immor	immer	always
99.6	pust	pust-	blow
.8	standbuild	Standbild	statue
.11	oertax	Ohr	ear
.11	sporran	Sporen	spurs
		sporen	dry up, rot
.16	drohneth svertgleam, Valkir lockt	droh-	threaten
		Schwert	sword
		lockt	beckons
.25	moliamordhar	Mord	murder
		Haar	hair
.27	rayheallach	lach-	laugh
100.5	Achdung!	Achtung!	attention!
		ach	oh
.5	Smucky	Schmuck	jewelry, decoration

.6	Pigeschoolies	geschul-	trained, schooled
.6 f	Lochlanner Fathach I	Loch	hole
	Fiounnisgehaven		
		ach	oh
		gehabt	had
		Hafen	harbour
.16	Centimachus'	mach-	make, do
.18	harauspices	Haar	hair
		heraus	out
		harus	(old Swiss battle-cry)
.19	innerhalf	innerhalb	inside
.19	zuggurat	Zucker	sugar
		Zug	train
		rat-	advise
		Rat	advice
.20	wyvern	Weibern	women
.22	litten	litten	suffered
.28	bauchspeech	Bauch	stomach
		Bauchredner	ventriloquist
.29	worldroom	Weltraum	space
.30	sammenlivers	zusammen	together
.36	Ulma	Ulm	elm (German city)
101.4	themses	Themse	Thames
.9	oom	Ohm	uncle
.9	ounckel	Onkel	uncle
		Enkel	grandchild
.17	aroof	Ruf	shout, cry
.19	yayas is yayas	ja	yes
.21	da! da!	da	there
.26 f	pratschkats	Prat (dial.)	babbling, talk
		Pratchen	story, anecdote
		Tratsch	gossip
		Katze	cat
.27	platschpails	plätschern	splash
		Platz	place
		platz-	split
.27	holenpolendom	holen	fetch
		Polen	Poland
		Dom	cathedral

.27 f	Szpaszpas	Spaß	joke, jollity
.33	murrmurr	murren	murmur, growl
.35	O ye!	o je!	oh dear!
102.4	rast	rast-	rest
.12	specks on her eyeux	Speck	bacon
		Eier	eggs
.19	balmheartzyheat	Barmherzigkeit	charity, mercy
.20	wort	Wort	word
.20	drogist	Drogist	druggist
.24	holden	hold	lovely
.28	pine	Pein	suffering
103.8	Nabuch	na	well
		Buch	book
104.10	*Treestam*	Stamm	(tree) trunk; tribe
.10	*Siseule*	Säule	column
		Eule	owl
.14	*Flur*	Flur	floor, meadow
.16 f	*hosebound*	Hosenband	trouser-belt, garter
.18	*Hoonsbood*	Huhn	chicken
	Hansbaad's	Bude	hut
		Hans	(German name)
		Bad	bath
.21	*Cammels*	Kamm	comb
105.1	*Plenge*	eng	narrow
.2	*Oremunds*	Ohr	ear
		Mund	mouth
.7	*Po*	Po	buttock
.9	*Taal*	Tal	valley
.9	*Taub*	taub	deaf
		Taube	dove
.11	*Intimier Minnelisp*	mir	to me
		Minne	love
.12	*Juckey*	juck-	itch
.14	*Allbart Noahnsy*	Bart	beard
		ahn-	suspect
		Ahn	grandfather, ancestor
.18	*Culpreints*	ein	one
		einst	once

.21	*Buckling*	Bückling	kipper
		Buckel	hump
.23	*Potstille*	Potz-	for God's-
		Stille	silence
		Postille	book of family
			sermons
.26	*Milchcow*	Milch	milk
.29	*Inn*	Inn	(river)
.33	*Battlewatschers*	Watsche	slap
.35 f	*Terriss*	Riß	tear
106.4	*Hustings*	husten	cough
.6	*Tonnoburkes*	Donner	thunder
.6	*Boob*	Bub	boy
.8	*Moohr*	Mohr	moor
		Ohr	ear
.9 f	*Brautchers*	Braut	bride
		Brautschauer	man looking for
			bride
.15	*Thonderhalt*	der	the
		bald	soon
.17	*Welikin's*	Wedekind	(author)
.24	*Popofetts*	Popo	buttocks
		fett	fat
.29	*Brahm*	Bram	broom
		Brahm-	Brahmin
		Brahm	(stage manager,
			critic)
		Rahm	cream
.31	*Blut*	Blut	blood
107.8	proteiform	Ei	egg
.9	alphabetters	Bett	bed
.15	lief	lief	ran
.36	hallhagal	Hagel	hail
		Hegel	(philosopher)
108.15	Elberfeld's	Elberfeld	(town)
		Elbe	(river)
		Feld	field
.25	kohol	Kohle	coal
109.1	cant	Kante	corner, edge
110.7	stern	Stern	star

.14	Zot	Zot-	obscenity
.21	Ahahn	Hahn	rooster
		ahn-	suspect
.22	fruur ... kuur	Frau	woman
		früher	earlier
		Kur	cure; election
.24	sahatsong	sah	saw
.31	mistridden	Mist	garbage, junk
.34	euchring	euch	you
.35	heily	heil!	hail!
		Heil	health, salvation
111.1	puteters	Pute	turkey-hen, conceited woman
.8	zogzag	zog	pulled
		zag-	hesitate
.17	twoinns	Inn	(river)
.18	ess	ess-	eat
.20	tache	Tasche	pocket
.32	boucher	Bauch	stomach
112.7	shoolerim	Schülerin	girl student
.29	Misthress	Mist	garbage, junk
113.3	Grabar	Gräber	graves
.12	schwants	Schwanz	tail
		Schwan	swan
.12	schwrites	Schweiz	Switzerland
.12	ischt	(Swiss pron. of) ist	is
.12	trootabout	Trut	turkey
.16	mollvogels	moll	minor (music)
		Vogel	bird
.18	inn	Inn	(river)
.19	held	Held	hero
.25	mein, ich beam ... fresch	mein	mine
		nein	no
		ich bin	I am
		frisch	fresh
114.4	Bukarahast	hast	(you) have
		Ast	branch
.5	Bulgarad	Rad	wheel

.6	schtschupnistling	Schuppe	(fish-) scale
		ist	is
		nisteln	nestle
.22	inhanger	Anhänger	trailer; adherent
.23	ous sot's	Aussatz	leprosy, itch
.25	gotsquantity	Gott	God
		Got-	goth
.28	messas	Messer	knife
.30	tag	Tag	day
115.17	awoh	wo	where
.21	and so wider	und so weiter	and so forth
.23	freudened	Freude	joy
.32	drauma	dräuen	threaten
		Traum	dream
		Raum	room
116.2 ff	meeter	Mieter	renter
.6 f	'Schottenboum'	Schotten	Scots
		Baum	tree
.21	moreinausland's	rein	in, clean
		ein	one
		aus	out
		Ausland	foreign country
.29	furtz	Furz	break wind
.32	ichabod, habakuk	ich	I
		hab-	have
		kuck-	look
117.4	Feueragusaria	Feuer	fire
.7	gruen	grün	green
.15	strassarab	Straße	street
.18	souffsouff	sauf-	drink
		Suff	swill
.18	claypot	Kleeblatt	clover leaf
.26	frier	frier-	freeze
.29	fersch	Ferse	heel
		fesch	stylish
118.15	who deeper thinks	(lit.) wer tiefer trinkt	he who drinks more
.21	Alle	alle	everyone, all
.34	lufted	Luft	air
119.2	Terracussa	Kuß	kiss

.8	stricly	Strick	rope, halter; scapegrace
		strick-	knit
.10	farmfrow's	Frau	woman, wife
.10	flayfell	Fell	skin
.19	sigla	Siegel	seal
.25	sansheneul	Eule	owl
.32	not?	Not	need, emergency
		nicht?	(used at end of question)
.36	or	Ohr	ear
120.3	wotty	Watte	cotton wool
.7 f	dummpshow	dumm	dumb
.31	kants koorts,	ganz kurz,	quite short,
	topplefouls	Doppelvau	letter W
.34	bornabarbar	ab	off
		bar	in cash
121.16	disdotted	Dis	D sharp (music)
.22	wetterhand	Wetter	weather
.26	selfsounder	(lit.) Selbstlaut	vowel
.36	toller	toller	madder
		Toller	(dramatist)
122.8	wrasted	rast-	rest
.10	fane's	Fahne	flag
.16	rossy	Roß	steed
123.9	sternly	Stern	star
.11	Duff-Muggli	Muggli	(little mosquito)
.18	*Forestallings over that Studium*	Vorstellungen über das Studium	conceptions of the study
.23	bestteller	bestell-	bespeak, order
		Teller	plate
.24	trianforan	voran	before, forwards
124.11	punct	Punkt	period, point
.15	Brotfressor	Brotfresser	bread-eater
.24 f	waterungspillfull	Wässerung	watering, dilution
		spiel-	play
.27	bisses	bis	to, until
		biß	bite
125.11	Formelly	formell	formal
		Formel	formula

.13	amuzement	Zement	cement
.16	persecussion	Kuß	kiss
126.4	briefdragger	Briefträger	postman
.12	buaboababbaun	Bub	boy
		Baum	tree
.15	chainganger's	Gang	going, motion, gait; gear (of motor); corridor
.17	lapapple	Pappel	poplar
.20	horthrug	Hort	hoard, safe retreat
.23	allmarken	Marken	stamps
.24	goflooded	ge-	(prefix for certain nouns, past participles)
127.1	toll	toll	mad
.4	fauss	Pfau	peacock
		Faust	fist
.10	F. E. R. T.	fertig	done, finished
		fährt	rides
.13	germhuns [Germans]	Germ	yeast
		Huhn	chicken
.13	besieged	besiegt	conquered, vanquished
.17	fraufrau's	Frau	woman, wife
.19	aas	Aas	carrion
.28	Indgangd	Eingang	entrance
.31	gehamerat	Geheimrat	privy councillor
.32	ernst	ernst	earnest
.32	mausey	Maus	mouse
.32	lustyg	lustig	merry
128.1	isst	ißt	eats
		ist	is
.2 f	quercuss	Querkopf	stubborn person
		quer	across
		Kuß	kiss
.5	hidal	Heidel-(beere)	whortleberry
		Heide	heathen
.5	hold	hold	gracious, lovely
.11	hose	Hose	trousers
.12	puder	Puder	powder

.26	Noolahn	Null	Zero
		Ahn	ancestor
		ahn-	suspect
129.1	wurstmeats	Wurst	sausage
.4	futter	Futter	feed
		Futt (vulg.)	vagina
		Vater	father
.4	magd	Magd	maid
.6	dank	Dank	thanks
.10	biguinnengs	eng	narrow
		Innung	craft-guild
.14	sollyeye	soll	should
		Ei	egg
.15	inn	Inn	(river)
.16	hausmann	Hausmann	tenant, lodger
.20	Rotshield	Rothschild	(family name)
		rot	red
		Schild	shield
.23	pigeonheim	Heim	home
.29	wassarnap	Wassernapf	water basin
130.3	yeladst	letzt	last, final
.5	reglar rack	regelrecht	regular, normal
.12	borgiess	borg-	borrow
		gieß-	pour
.12	bier	Bier	beer
.13	Roh	roh	raw, crude
.15	hockinbechers	hocken	crouch, squat
		Becher	beaker, mug
.16	das	das	the, that
.20	hickheckhocks	Heck	rear (of a car), fence, stern
		hocken	crouch, squat
.21	binn	bin	am
.27	girther, girther and girther	größer	larger
131.4	Diener	Diener	servant
.7	evrywehr	Wehr	defence, corps
.7	morder	Mörder	murderer
.7	Ostman	Ost	East
.8	baases	Base	female cousin, aunt

.11	saulely	Säule	column, pillar
.15	repunked	Punkt	period
.19	unsightliness	(lit.) Unsicht-barkeit	invisibility
.25	curach	Kur	cure
		ach!	oh!
.28	morvenlight	Möwen	seagulls
132.14	toll	toll	mad
.23	lout	laut	loud
.24	mareschalled	Marschall	marshall
		Schall	resonance
.25	grossed	groß	large
.29	orege	rege	lively
.29	lachsembulger	Lachs	salmon
	[Luxemburger]		
		lach-	laugh
		Achse	axis
.32	tarnpike	tarn-	camouflage
.35	gorky	Gurke	cucumber, pickle
.36	comm, eilerdich	komm	come
		eile dich	hurry up
133.1	stark	stark	strong
.6	Riesengebirger	Riesengebirge	(Giant Mountains: Sudetic range)
.8	hose	Hose	trousers
.8	taut sheets	Tauchnitz	(publisher)
		taut	melts
.8 f	mack Liebsterpet	mach	make, do
		Liebster	dearest
.16	Matrosenhosens	Matrosen	sailors
		Hosen	trousers
.21 f	Ubermeerschall	über	over
	Blowcher	Meer	sea
		Schall	resonance, echo
		Blücher	(Prussian general)
.27	shoebard	Schubert	(composer)
.29	schenkt	schenkt	pours, gives
		Schenke	pub
.29	brigstoll	Stolle	cake
		toll	mad

.29 f	drey orchafts	drei	three
		Ortschaft	village, place
.31	lebriety	leb-	live
		Leber	liver
134.1	Baulacleeva	Bau	building, construction
		Klee	clover
.7	damimonds	Dame	lady
		Mond	moon
.7 f	fear of spates; cumbrum, cumbrum	vier	four
		Spaten	spade
		brumm-	grumble, buzz
		spät	late
.8	drum	drum	therefore
.22	bewitthered	Gewitter	weather, storm
		Witwe	widow
		wittert	smells
135.1	melking	melken	milk
.1	murry	mürrisch	surly, morose
		murr-	grumble, growl
.3	hose	Hose	trousers
.4	foretellers	(lit.) Vorsager	prompter
		Teller	plate
.6	annacrwatter	Watte	cotton wool
		Krawatte	necktie
.10	Barth-	Bart	beard
.22	decks	deck-	cover, decorate
.25	Ostenton	Osten	east
		Enten	ducks
		Ton	sound, tone
.32	links lock	links	leftward
		lock-	beckon, allure
.36	saggarts	sag-	say
		Art	kind, sort
136.8	Ostrov	Ost	east
.13	fjeld	Feld	field
.15	Osterich	Ost	east
		Österreich	Austria

.21	Tortur	Tor	fool; door, gate
		Tür	door
.24	heft	Heft	notebook; handle
.28	loeven	Löwen	lions
.31 f	Koenigstein's	König	king
		Stein	stone
		Königstein	(Saxonian town)
137.1	succar	Zucker	sugar
.12	Kukkuk	Kuckuck	cuckoo
.31	rooksacht	Rucksack	rucksack
		Ruck	jolt
		sacht	soft, gently
138.1	himmeltones	Himmel	heaven, sky
.8	motts	Motte	moth
.12	beeter	Bieter	bidder
		Beete	beds (of flowers)
		Beter	one who prays
.13	fritz	Fritz	(name)
.13	beschotten	Schotten	partitions, bulk-
			heads; Scotsmen
		beschossen	shot at
.18	badend	badend	bathing
.20	Inn	Inn	(river)
.23	Ebblannah	nah	near
.27	predikants	Kant-	edge, corner
		Predigt	sermon
.32	hahnreich	Hahn	rooster
		reich	rich; empire, reign;
			(suffix equivalent
			to -dom)
		Hahnrei	cuckold
.33	althe	Alte	old person
.34	shricked	Schrei	cry, scream
		erschrickt	is terrified
.34	weibduck	Weib	female
139.3	blick	Blick	look
.3	saumon	Sau	sow (pig)
		Saum	seam, hem
.8	stehts	steh-	stand
		stets	steadily, always

.15	mutter	Mutter	mother
.20	bergs	Berg	mountain
.32	magda	Magd	maid
.33	Whorort	wo	where
		hör	hear
		Ort	place, village
		Vorort	suburb
.33	Ousterholm	Auster	oyster
.33	Dreyschluss	Drei (Arch.: drey)	three
		Schluß	conclusion, end
.36	Wohn	wohn-	live, reside
.36	Roomyeck	Ruhm	fame
		Eck	corner
141.5	Shalldoll	Schall	sound, echo
.6	Shand	Schande	shame, disgrace
.8	retten	retten	save
.9	melk	melk-	milk
.12	foottreats	Fußtritt	kick
.14	underhold	(Lit.) Unterhalt	maintenance, livelihood
		Unhold	monster
.14	putzpolish	putz-	clean, polish
		Putz	finery, attire
.17	spoorwaggen	Spur	track, trace
		Wagen	car, wagon
.21	begripe full- standingly irers'	begreif vollständig ihr	comprehend fully their
.22	kine	kein	no
.23	earnst	ernst	earnest
.25	pershoon	Huhn	chicken, hen
.31	claub	klau-	steal
		Laub	foliage
		klaube-	pick out, cull
142.3	mowlding	Maul	mouth, snout
		Ding	thing
.12	prater	Prater	(Vienna district)
.27	Barty	Bart	beard
143.1	hose hol'd	Hose	trousers
		hol-	get, fetch
.13	reconjungation	jung	young

.22	starring	starr	stiff, rigid
		starr-	stare
.25	gelb	gelb	yellow
.34	achamed	ach	oh
144.2	got	Gott	god
.6	Prendregast	Gast	visitor, customer
.7	Innkipper	Inn	(river)
		kippen	tip, capsize
.7	maulers	Maul	mouth, snout
.10	Eilish	eil-	hurry
		eilig	speedy, hurried
.12	Andoo musnoo	du	you
		muß	must
		nu	now
145.6	Angst	Angst	fear, anxiety
.7 f	mishymissy	misch-	mix
.21	Transname	(lit.) übernehmen	take over
.26	leib	Leib	body
.34	sonnamonk	Sonne	sun
146.12	Schwipps	schwipp	nimble, pliant
		Schwips	drunk
.13	Ballshossers	Schoß	shot; sprig; lap, bosom
.16	gleison	Gleis	tracks, rails
.35	Garnd . . . mand	Garn	thread
		Mandel	almond
.36	I go you before	Ich gehe dir vor	I will precede you
147.6	Nicholls	Hölle	hell
.11	Hoost! Ahem!	husten	cough
.11	Bett	Bett	bed
.32	pouder	Puder	powder
148.2	*Misi, misi*	mies	weakly, bad
.23	cantalang	Kante	edge, corner
		Tal	valley
		lang	long
.26	muss whiss	muß wissen	must know
.29	frucht	Frucht	fruit
149.5	mundy	Mund	mouth
.7	lech	lechzen	gape, languish
		Lech	(river)

.9	to wiles	zuweilen	occasionally
.19	Schott	Schott-	Scot
.24	Schott	Schott-	Scot
150.5	Talis von Talis	Tal	valley
		von	of
.5	funk	Funk-	spark
.9	Ubeleeft	übel	evil, bad, sick
.10	Suchman's	such	search
		man	one
			(impers.
			pronoun)
.11	fatter of macht	Vater	father
		Macht	might, power
		machst	does, makes
.11	Gedankje	Gedanke	thought
.12 f	While thou beast'	Weil du bist ein	because you are a
	one zoom of a	Sohn der Welt	son of the world
	whorl!		
.15	Loewy-Brueller	Löwe	lion
		brüll-	roar
.16	Sennacherib	Senn-	cowherd
		nach	after
		nachher	later
.17	Skekels	Ekel	nausea, disgust
.27	Feigenbaumblatt	feig	cowardly
		Feigenbaum	fig tree
		Blatt	leaf
151.8	obintentional	ob	whether
		oben	above
.12	-Eitelnaky	eitel	vain
.14	astensably	Ast	branch
.19	*Mitleid*	Mitleid	pity
.29	lequou	leck-	lick
.31	meinungs	Meinung	opinion
.33	Bryllars	brüll-	roar
		Brille	eye glasses
.35	Mine, dank	mein	my
		nein	no
		Dank	thank
152.18	Eins	eins	one

.18	wohned	wohn-	live, reside
.19	onesomeness	(lit.) einsam	lonely
153.1	secunding	Sekunde	second
.6	rinn	rinn-	fun, flow
.18 f	brooder-on-low	Bruder	brother
.23	Room	Ruhm	fame
.24	satt	satt	full, satisfied
.25	poposterously	Popo	buttocks
.27	wouest	Wüste	desert, waste
.29	frisherman's	frisch	fresh
.31	fetter	fett	fat
		Vetter	cousin
.31	summe	Summe	sum
		summe	hum, buzz
154.5	liseias	Lise	Lizzie
		sei	be
		Ei	egg
.8 f	robenhauses	Haus	house
.18	mund	Mund	mouth
.19	nase	Nase	nose
.34	stockend	stockend	hesitatingly
		Stock	stick, mould
155.5 f	Novarome	warum	why
.6	bleives	Blei	lead
.19	mein goot	mein Gott	my God
		gut	good
.23	peint	Pein	pain
.23	blick	Blick	look, glance
.30	dry and drysick	drei-und-dreißig	thirty-three
.36	ehrltogether	Ehr-	honor
156.1	alter	Alter	age
.12	sarchnaktiers	Sarg	coffin
		nackt	naked
		Akt	nude model
		Tier	animal
.21	amsered	Amse (dial.)	ant
.30	Nuzuland	nu zu Land	now to land
.34	mear's	mir	me
.35	Unsightbared	(lit.) unsichtbar	invisible

.36	Hourihaleine	alleine	alone
		Leine	leash
		eine	one (femin.)
157.11	glaubering hochskied	Glaube	belief
		Hochzeit	wedding
.11	welkinstuck	welken	wither
		Stock	stick
		Stuck	stucco
.12	zwivvel	Zweifel	doubt
.15	Fuerst	Fürst	prince
		erst	first
.28	damprauch	Dampf	steam
		Rauch	smoke
.28	buchstubs	Buchstaben	letters (of alphabet)
158.4	obliviscent	ob	whether
		wissend	knowing
.5	menner	Männer	men
.7	grose	große	large
.12 f	he could not all hear	(Gm. word order)	
.14	trit	Tritt	kick
		tritt	tread, step
.16	undths	und	and
		uns	we
.17	Gri feeled	greif-	grab
		viel	many, much
.17	grice	Greis	old man
.23	wecking	wecken	wake up
.30	boshop's	boshaft	malicious
159.1	shieling	schielen	squint
.5	saule	Sau	sow (pig)
		Säule	column
.17	*Weh, O weh!*	Weh, O weh	woe is me
.31	theabild	Bild	picture, icon
160.9	stand	Stand	condition
.14	hockery	hock-	crouch, squat
		höckerig	hunchbacked
.27	billfaust	Faust	fist
.29	faust	Faust	fist
.31	Shultroj	Schule	school
		Schulter	shoulder

.31	Kiel	Kiel	keel
161.3	*Bettlermensch*	Bettler	beggar
		Mensch	person
.6	intellecktuals	leckt	licks
.12	Caseous	Käse	cheese
.12 f	seemaultaneously	Maul	mouth, muzzle
.16	milkstoffs	Stoff	material, cloth
.18	Caseous	Käse	cheese
.23	Schott	Schott-	Scot
.24	Mutti . . . Mutti	Mutti	mother, mommy
.25	suppy	Suppe	soup
.27	Slatbowel	Salat	salad, lettuce
.27	Pfarrer	Pfarrer	parson
.28	Pedersill	Petersilie	parsley
.33	Schott	Schott-	Scot
162.4	juke	juck-	itch
.9	plankrieg	Krieg	war
		krieg-	get
.17	weste	Weste	vest
.19	inessive	ess-	eat
.19	kezom	Käse	cheese
.20	hazzy	Hase	hare
.21	hazbane	Hase	hare
.28	semagen	Magen	stomach
.30	seeingscraft	Kraft	power, ability
.32	augstritch	Auge	eye
		Strich	line, stroked
.33	younker	Junker	country squire
163.3	salm	Salm	psalm, sermon
.5 ff	*Der Haensli ist ein Butterbrot, mein Butterbrot! Und Koebi iss dein Schtinkenkot! Ja! Ja! Ja!*	(German as written with pun on iss-ist and Schinken-brot-Stinkend-kot)	Little Hans is a piece of buttered bread, my buttered bread! And Koebi (Jacob) eat/is your ham sandwich/ stinking filth. Yes! Yes! Yes!
.8	Caseous	Käse	cheese
.10	wurms	Wurm	worm

.25	swoors	Schwur	oath, swore
.26	whiles	weil	because
164.11	platinism	Platin	platinum
.24	Caseous	Käse	cheese
.31	Herr	Herr	Mr.
165.7	Bdur	B dur	B major
.9	tonehall	Tonhalle	concert hall (the one in Zurich bears that name)
.10	breaf	Brief	letter
.12	Caseous	Käse	cheese
166.15	brieffrocked	Brief	letter
.36	Caseous	Käse	cheese
167.4	-Caseous	Käse	cheese
.19	nefand	Neffe	nephew
		Pfand	pawn
		fand	found
168.4	welling	Wellen	waves
169.4	Blaubarb	blau	blue
170.6	yungfries	Jungfrau	virgin
		Jungfer	maid
.16	abblokooken	ab	off
		Kuchen	cake
.21	looft	Luft	air
.24	rocks	Rock	skirt, jacket
.26	Gibsen's	gib's	give it
.28	lax	Lachs	salmon
.29	gaffed	Gaffel	fork
		gafft	gapes
.31	Ananias'	Ananas	pineapple
.32	Englend	eng	narrow
171.1	Rosbif	Roß	steed
		Rost	roast
.6	Irrland's	irr	mad, mistaken
.11	czitr	zitter-	shiver
		Zither	zither
.14	brewbarrett	Bart	beard
		rett-	save
		Barett	beret

.17	funkleblue	Funk	spark
		funkel-	sparkle
		leb-	live
		kleb-	stick
.24	jo . . . jo, jo	ja	yes
.25	jo jo jo	ja	yes
.27	feherbour	Feh	miniver
		Fieber	fever
.31 f	Tulloch-Turnbull	Loch	hole
		turn-	do gymnastics
.32	shotted	Schott-	Scot
			bulkhead
		Schote	sheet, pod, husk
.36 f	nummer	Nummer	number
172.1	tren	trenn-	divide, separate
.22	maulth	Maul	mouth, muzzle
.31	Munda	Mund	mouth
.36	dem	dem	to him, to it
173.1	sousy	saus-	storm, rush
.10	lauscher	Lauscher	listener
.13	Albiogenselman	Gänse	geese
.13	bin	bin	am
.15	samtalaisy	Samt	velvet
		Tal	valley
.19	swrine	rein	pure, clean
.27	Himmyshimmy	Himmel	sky, heaven
		Schimmel	white horse
		Himmel-Schimmel	(expletive)
174.29 f	laetich	ich	I
175.5	Nichil	nicht	not
.12	*Sachsen*	Sachsen	Saxony
.12	*Judder*	Jude	jew
.16	*Arcobaleine*	allein	alone
	forespoken	Leine	leash, rope
		eine	one
		(lit.) vorsprechen	pronounce, announce
.17	*Hempal*	Himmel	heaven
.17	*tumpel*	Tümpel	pool, puddle
.22	*Bier*	Bier	beer

.23	*laff*	Affe	monkey
		Laffe	fop, dandy
.25	*dumm*	dumm	dumb, stupid
176.23	roth, vice and blause	rot	red
		weiß	white
		blau	blue
.25 f	rank funk	Rundfunk	radio
.27	Talviland	Tal	valley
.33 f	whole bach	Holbach	(philosopher)
		Bach	brook
.35	Schwitzer's	Schwytzer	Swiss man
		schwitz-	sweat
177.2	tarned	tarn-	camouflage, mask
.10	chems	(German pronunciation of *jam*)	
.22	Bethgelert	gelehrt	learned, taught
		geleert	emptied,poured out
178.2	fad	fad	stale, dull
.6	alley	alle	all
.7	spuking	spucken	spit
		spuken	haunt
.10	erstborn	erst	first
.15	waaded	wate	wade
		Wade	calf
.15	baaded	baden	bathe
.28	durdicky	dur	major (music)
		dick	fat, thick
.29	Nassaustrass	naß	wet
		Saus	storm
		aus	out
		Straße	street
.30	wetter	Wetter	weather
		wett-	bet
.35	Duvvelsache	Sache	thing, cause
179.7	hosed	Hose	pants
.32	roseschelle	Esche	ashtree
		Schelle	bell
180.3	probscenium	Probe	rehearsal, try
.5	acountstrick	Strick	rope, halter
		strick-	knit

.5	im	im	in the
.7	loutgout	Laut	tone, sound
		laut	loud
8.	Baraton McGluckin	Ton	tone
		Glocken	bells
		Glück	luck
.25	rot	rot	red
181.3	Spache	Sprache	language, speech
.4	schicker	schick-	send
		Schick	tact, due order
.4	Pioupioureich	Reich	kingdom, country
		reich	rich
.5	Swabspays	Schwabe	Swabian (Swiss for German man)
.6	Danubierhome	Bier	beer
.19	Futt	Futter	fodder
		Futt (sl.)	vagina
182.9	zinnzabar	Zinn	tin, pewter
		Zins	interest
		bar	cash
.27	moostarshes	Moos	moss
183.5 f	Niggs, niggs, and niggs	nichts	nothing
184.2	jas jos	ja, jo	yes
.16	lallaryrook	lall-	stammer, lisp
.19	frulling	Frühling	spring
.22	Asther's	Ast	branch
.22	Huster's	hust-	cough
.24	regale	Regale	shelves
.27	avgs	Auge	eye
.28	Meinfelde	mein	my
		Felde	field
.28	eiers	Eier	eggs
.31	toyast	Ast	branch
185.3	Podex	Podex	posterior
.4	Flammeus	Flamme	flame
.27	firman	Firmen	companies, firms
.29	nichthemerically	nicht	not
.34	Menschavik	Mensch	person
186.11	arklyst	Arglist	deceit, artifice

.19	Kruis-	Kreis	circle, district
.29	rand	Rand	edge
.31	boardelhouse	Bordell	brothel
	fongster	Fenster	window
.32	meansort herring	meine Herren	gentlemen!
.35	clutcharm	klatsch-	applaud
		Arm	arm
.36	Purtsymessus	Purzel	tumble
187.3	stummung	stumm	dumb
		Stimmung	atmosphere
.3	sake	Sache	case
.4	burstteself	Bürste	brush
.10	outgift	ausgeben	spend
		Ausgabe	edition
.15	Polthergeist-kotzdondherhoploits	Poltergeist	hobgoblin
		kotz-	vomit
		Donner und Blitz	thunder and lightning!
.25	breit	breit	broad
.27	Baus	Bau	building
		aus	out
		bauz!	smash
.33	zwilling	Zwilling	twin
188.15	forenenst	nennst	(you) mention
.31	Abgott	Abgott	idol
189.12	minneful	Minne	love
.18	Sorge	Sorge	worry, sorrow (dramatist)
190.2	stphruck	Frack	tuxedo
		Ruck	jerk
.36	mus	Mus	sauce
		muß	must
191.4	Afferyank	Affe	monkey
.6	tilyet	(lit.:) bis jetzt	until now
.10	-am-Bummel	am	at the
		Bummel	stroll
.17	celebesty	lebest	(you) live
.35	bourgeoismeister	Bürgermeister	mayor
.35 f	himmels	Himmel	sky, heaven

.36	punt	Punkt	point, period
.36	wishywashy	weiße Wäsche	laundry, underwear
192.8	schamer	Scham	shame
.30	selene	Seele	soul
.30 f	lightthrowers	(lit.:) Scheinwerfer	headlamps, searchlights
.36	balbettised	Bett	bed
193.5	mux	Mucks	slight sound
.13	Herr	Herr	Mister
194.6	spiritus	Spiritus	alcohol
.30	beck	Beck (dial.)	baker
.31	tachie	Tasche	pocket, handbag
196.11	reppe	Repe	(river)
.15	saale	Saale	(river)
.20	loch	Loch	hole
		Locha	(river)
.24	rappe	Rappen	black horse; Swiss cent
197.4	wiesel	Wiesel	weasel
		wie	how
		Wiese	meadow; (river)
		Esel	donkey
.7	elster	Elster	(river)
.8	Caput	kaputt	broken
.9	Urgothland	Ur-	original, primitive
.11	blocksmitt	mit	with
.11	saft	Saft	juice
.21	asthore	Ast	branch
		höre	hear
.26	waag	Waage	scale
		Waag	(river)
		wag-	dare
.35	bowmpriss	Baum	tree
		riß	tore
		iß	eat
.35	borst	Borste	bristle
.35	bar	bar	in cash
198.4	ruhring	Ruh	rest
		Ruhr	(district); (river)
		rühren	stir, move

.5	spree	Spree	(river)
.5	buah	Bua (dial. for Bube)	boy
.5	erned	er	he
.7	kaldt	kalt	cold
.8	Wasserbourne	Wasser	water
.13	limmat	Limmat	(river)
.18	emme	Emme	(river)
.18	reussischer	Reuse	oyster-basket
		russischer	Russian
		Reuß	(river)
.23	windaug	Aug-	eye
		Vindach	(river)
.26	bogans	Bogen	bow
.27	Tista suck	(dial.) ist a' Sach'	It's as follows!
			What an affair!
.29	glommen	glomm	glimmered
.31	allbrant	Alprand	edge of mountains
.34	drammen	Dramen	plays
.35	drommen	Drommet	trumpet
		Dremme	(river)
199.3	swolf	zwölf	twelve
.7	sternes	Stern	star
.7	zwarthy	zwar	indeed
.12	Wendawanda	Wende	(river)
		Wande	(river)
.18	Kaffue mokau an	Kaffee	coffee
		Mokka	mocca
		kauen	chew
.19 f	shinkobread	Schinkenbrot	ham sandwich
.22	russ	Ruß	soot
.23	metauwero rage	Tau	dew
		wer	who
		rage	loom, tower (verbs)
.24	rieses	Riese	giant
.24	kast	Kasten	box
.24	frome	fromm	pious
.26	platteau	Platt-	disk, platter
		platt	flat, vulgar
.34	gebroren	geboren	born

.35	dochter	doch	yet
		Docht	wick
		Tochter	daughter
.35 f	funkling	Funk-	spark
		funkeln	sparkle
200.4	porpor	purpur	crimson
.4	brahming	Brahm	(stage manager, critic)
.6	poother	Pute	turkey hen
.8 f	waterglucks	glucks-	gurgle
		Glück	luck
.11	hoon var	Huhn war	hen was
.29	neiss	Neisse	(river)
.30	inny	Inn	(river)
.31	pleissful	Pleis	(river)
.32	hab	hab-	have
.35	flut	Flut	flood
.36	lerryn	lehren	teach
201.1	rede	Rede	speech, talk
.2	tummel	tummeln	turn around, hurry, prance
.3	Tarn	tarn-	mask, camouflage
.4	ore	Ohr	ear
.4	Essonne inne	essen	eat
		Sonne	sun
		inne-	within
.18	*plage*	Plage	plague, bother
.23	jagsthole	Jagst	(river)
.25	bundukiboi	Bund	union, bunch
.25	meet	mit	with
.26	Inns	Inn	(river)
.28	rede	rede	speech, speak
.33	Kund	kund	known
.34	Eyolf	elf	eleven
.35	Pluhurabelle	Hure	prostitute
.35	loreley	Lorelei	(Siren on the Rhine)
202.2	neins	nein	no
.7	cam	kam	came

.8	neckar	Neckar	(river)
		neck-	tease
.10	tilhavet	Havel	(river)
.18	hosting	husten	cough
.19	Nieman	niemand	nobody
.19	Nirgends	nirgends	nowhere
.20	Albern	albern	silly, foolish
.32	forstfellfoss	Forst	forest
		Fell	skin, hide
.36	nullahs	null	zero
203.7	wellingtonorseher	Seher	seer
.8 f	Wasut	Was ist?	what's wrong?
.14	Neya	ja	yes
.16	ferse	Ferse	heel
.17	dinkel	dunkel	dark
		Dinke	(river)
.18	heremite	Eremit	hermit
.28	galbs	gelb	yellow
.28	indergoading	Inder	Indian
.29	vierge	vier	four
.31	elfun	elf	eleven
204.1	hielt	hielt	held
.2	souff'	sauf-	drink, guzzle
.12	poing	Po	posterior
.22	flenders	flenn-	whine
.28	Rother	rot	red
.34	oder	oder	or
		Oder	(river)
205.10	seifety	Seife	soap
.15	amstel	Amsel	ousel
.17	Wakeschrift	Wochenschrift	weekly magazine
.23	erriff	Riff	ridge, reef
		er rief	he called
.25	Inn	Inn	(river)
.25	Jude's	Jude	jew
.27	etsched	Etsch	(river)
.29 f	Evropeahahn cheic	Hahn	rooster
		Ei	egg
.32	peihos	Ei	egg
		Hos-	pants

.34	-Meer	Meer	sea
.35	Hausman	Hausmann	tenant, lodger
206.1	mauldrin	Maul	mouth, muzzle
		drin	inside
.3	Hing	hing	hung
.8	niever	nie	never
.9	bergened	bergen	recover, conceal
.10	mailsack	Mehlsack	bag of flour
.15 f	Minneha, minnehi	Minne	love
	minaaehe, minneho	Ehe	marriage
.26	scheldt	schelt-	scold
		Schelde	(river)
.29	flussed	Fluß	river
.31	fraguant	frag-	ask
.31	wupper	Wupper	(river)
.31	lauar	lau-	luke- (warm)
		auf der Lauer	lurking, in ambush
		Lauer	(river)
207.7	rhunerhinerstones	Rhein	(river)
.9	lippeleens	Lippe	(river)
.12	Ciliegia	lieg-	lie
.12	Kirschie	Kirsche	cherry
		Kirsch	brandy
.13	respecks	Speck	bacon
.15	sprizzling	spritz-	squirt, spray
.19	shulder	schuld	blame, guilty
		Schulter	shoulder
.19	bassein	sein	be
.21	Spitz	spitz	pointed, sharp
.23	mosel	Mosel	(river)
.35	ems	Ems	(river)
.36	aues	Aue	meadow
208.1	elb	Elbe	(river)
.2	werra	Werra	(river)
.10	fishnetzeveil	Netze	nets
		netz-	moisten
		Veilchen	violet
.13	tinto	Tinte	ink
.15	bockknickers	Bock	kid, he-goat, beer
		nick-	nod

.20	alpheubett	Heu	hay
		Bett	bed
.26	ffiffty	pfiff	whistled
.26	lungarhodes	Ungar	Hungarian
		gar	cooked
		Hode	testicle
.31	hex	Hexe	witch
.35	recknitz	Regnitz	(river)
209.7	aneber	neben	next to
.18	arundgirond	rund	around, round
.22	weser	Weser	(river)
		Wiese	meadow
		Wesen	being
.22	edereider	Eder	(river)
		Eider	(river)
.25	Reims	Reim	rhyme
.26	lech	Lech	(river)
.27	aisch	Aisch	(river)
.28	gabe	Gabe	gift
.31	paunschaup	schau	look
.34	vicereine's	rein	pure
		eine	one
.34	Annchen	Annchen	little Ann
210.2	raabed	Rabe	raven
		Raab	(river)
.2	meerschaundize	Meerschaum	meerschaum
		Meer	sea
		Schaum	foam
		schauen	look
.3	aringarung	Erinnerung	remembrance
.6	buch	Buch	book
.28	reiz	Reiz	attraction, irritation
.32	Arhone	Ahorn	maple
.35	niester	Niester	(river)
		niest	sneezes
		nie	never
		Nester	nests
211.1	Mann	Mann	man
.1	starr	starr	stiff

.7	penteplenty	Pente	(river)
.16 f	Rubiconstein	Stein	stone
.19	varians muck	Schmuck	jewelry, ornament
.23	Livienbad	Bad	bath
.24	spas	Spaß	merriment
.25	ills	Ill	(river)
.27	hempen	Hemden	shirts
.28	Conditor	Konditor	candy-maker
.36	-silvier	vier	four
212.4	Rossa	Roß	steed
.8	Kieran	kehren	sweep, turn
.8	Lappin	Lappen	rag
.8	Zusan	zu	to, shut
.10	Lezba	letz-	rejoice, gratify
.11	Rohan	roh	raw
.26	mulde	Mulde	trough, depression
.27	reckitts	reck-	stretch
		Kitt	putty
.27	lohaned	Loh-	blaze, flame
.36 f	*Die Windermere*	die	the
	Dichter	Dichter	poet
.2	*Floss*	Floß	raft
		floß	flowed
213.2	Ja	ja	yes
.2 f	Altmuehler	alt	old
		Mühle	mill
		Altmühl	(river)
.8	maure	Mauer	wall
.9	Regn onder	Regen	rain
		der	the
.10	for mere	für	for
		mir	me
.11	kennet	kenne	know
.14	Fieluhr	(wie) viel Uhr	what time is it?
.15	senne	Senne	cowherd
.17	bach	Bach	brook
.19	Sexaloitez	Sechseläuten	Zurich spring festival
.20	showers	Schauer	shudder
.23	Der went	der Wind	the wind

.30	Mutter	Mutter	mother
.30	Wharnow	Warne	(river)
.30	alle	alle	all
214.2	main	Main	(river)
.8	ufer . . . ufer	Ufer	bank, shore
.8	respund	Spund	bung, plug
		und	and
.9	irrawaddyng	irr	mad, aimless
.9	aars	Aar	(river)
.12	forehengist	Reh	doe
		Hengst	stallion
		ist	is
.12	Otters	Otter	(river)
.13	Isset	iß	eat
.22	creakorheuman bitts	Heu	hay
		bitt-	ask, plead
.28	limpopo	Popo	buttocks
.30	I sar	Isar	(river)
215.3	Indes	indes	in that, while
.4	Die . . . die	die	the
.13	trinkettoes	trink	drink
		Kette	chain
.13	buntz	bunt	colored, bright
.14	foostherfather	Fuß	foot
		ost	east
.23	seim	Seim	mucilage; honey
		sei	be
.31	chittering	zitter-	tremble
		Zither	zither
.31 f	Flittering	Flitter	tinsel
		flittern	flit, glitter
.34	foos . . . moos	Fuß	foot
		Moos	moss
		Mus	sauce, jam
.35	elm	Elm	(river)
.36	halls	hall-	resound, echo
216.3	elm	Elm	(river)
219.2	Feenichts	Feen	fairies
		nichts	nothing
.9	Genesius	genes-	recover, grow well

.11	Coarbs	Korb	basket
.12	Sollis	soll	should
.12	Dusort	du	you
		Ort	place
.13	Sennet	Senne	cowherd
.18	fern	fern	distant
.18	firn	firn	of last year, old
		Firn	mountain top
220.25	Schweden	Schweden	Sweden
221.6	Oelsvinger	Oel	oil
.9	geyswerks	Werk	factory, work
.10	scherinsheiner	Scheren	scissors
		Schein	appearance, light
.15	aasgaars	Aas	bait, carrion
		Aasgeier	vulture
.20	beorbtracktors	Beauftragter	deputy
.23	Hexenschuss	Hexenschuß	(lit.) witch-shot; lumbago
.23 f	Rocknarrag	Narr	fool
.25	Coollimbeina	Bein	leg
		beinah	almost
.29	Toll	toll	mad
.30	Morgen	Morgen	morning, tomorrow
.32	doofpoosts	doof	stupid, tiresome
		pust-	blow
.33	Wohntbedarft	wohnt	lives, resides
		Bedarf	requirement
		Wohnbedarf	home furnishings
.33	oakmulberryeke	Bereich	district, field
.34	Grabstone	Grabstein	gravestone
222.3	hirtly	Hirt	herdsman
.10 f	Oh Off Nunch Der Rasche Ver Lasse Mitsch Nitscht	Oh Hoffnung der Rache, verlasse mich nicht!	Oh hope of revenge, abandon me not!
		Der Rasche	the quick one
		misch-	mix
		mit	with
		Nische	niche
.12 f	Baretherootsch	rutsch-	slide

.18	Neid	Neid	envy
.26	Punct	Punkt	point, period
.28	liubbocks	Lübeck	(city)
		Bock	ram, he-goat
.28	kelchy	Kelch	chalice, cup
.29	clayblade	Kleeblatt	clover leaf
.33	zitterings	zitter-	tremble
		Zither	zither
223.5	Mutther	Mutter	mother
.8	jawr	ja	yes
		Jahr	year
.12	stulpled	Stulp-	brim, cuff
		Tölpel	country idiot, yokel
		stolp-	stumble
.21	dumm	dumm	stupid
.26	feinder	Feind	enemy
.27	worden schall	(ge)worden	became
		Schall	echo, sound
.29	untergone	unter	under
		untergehen	submerge, fail
.30	luft	Luft	air
.31	bloomingrund	Blumen	flowers
		Grund	ground, land;
			reason; bottom
		rund	round
224.7	roust	raus	out
.7	meast	mies	bad
		Ast	branch
.7	Atem	Atem	breath
.8	ourtales	Urteil	judgment, decision
.11	inhebited	heb-	lift, elevate
.12	hehry antlets	hehr	majestic, sublime
		Ehre	honor
		Antlitz	visage, face
		letz-	rejoice, gratify
.14	interregnation	Regen	rain
.18	morrder	Mörder	murderer
.19	vogalstones	Vogel	bird
.20	flooting	Flut	flood
.26	fand	fand	found

.31	braught	Brau	brew
		Braut	bride
		Brauch	custom
		braucht	needs
.31	angskt	Angst	fear
.34	hold	hold	lovely
.35 f	Hast thou feel liked	Hast du vielleicht	have you perhaps
225.2	wordchary	(lit.) wortkarg	taciturn
.2	atvoiced	(lit.) bestimmt	certainly
.4	harff	Harfe	harp
.10	ankered	Anker	anchor
		kehr-	turn, sweep
.13 f	worrawarrawurms	Worms	(city)
		Wurm	worm
.16	can	kenn-	know
.16	golten	Gold	gold
		gelten	be worth, be valid
.20	wolly	woll-	want
		Wolle	wool
.24	Hellfeuersteyn	helf-	help
		euer	your
		Feuer	fire
		Stein	stone
		Feuerstein	flint
.35 f	The flossies all and mossies all they drooped upon her draped brimfall. The bowknots, the showlots, they . . .		(structure of German song, „Die Vogelhochzeit")
226.6	Woefear	wofür	what for
.26	fomefing	fing	caught
.36	Dies	dies	this
227.5	helts	hält's	holds
		Held	hero
.20	monatan	Monaten	months
.21	woad	Wut	anger, madness
.35	tastarin	tast-	touch, feel

.36	imbretellated	im	in
		Brettl	skis
228.1	Machonochie	mach-	make, do
.4	Macnoon	mach' nun	do now
.5	mag	mag	like, may
.6	Seek hells	Sieg heil	(Nazi cheer)
.7	Mocknitza	mag' nits	(dial.) don't like
			anything
		mach nichts	do nothing
.7	Genik	Genick	neck
		genug	enough
.14	schlucefinis	Schluß	finish, end
.14	Gelchasser	Kelch	chalice
		Haß	hate
.14	Mischnary	misch-	mix
.17	Unkel	Unke	toad, grumbler
.21	heissrohgin	heiß	hot; is called
		roh	raw
.22	absendee	absenden	send off, mail
.23	farecard	Fahrkarte	ticket (for travel)
.24	getrennty	getrennt	separated
.28	Fuisfinister	Fenster	window
		finster	dark
.35	Ladigs	ledig	unmarried
.36	tinsammon	zusammen	together
229.3	Gout strap Fenlanns	Gott strafe England	May God punish
			England
.4	vineshanky's	Weinschank	wine-shop
	schwemmy	Schwemme	tavern
.16	Walpurgas Nackt	Walpurgis Nacht	Walpurgis night
		nackt	naked
.17 f	Leimuncononnulstria	Leim	glue
.18	globbtrottel	Trottel	cretin, fool
.22	gummer	Kummer	sorrow
.23	cluft	Kluft	cleft, chasm
		Luft	air
.25	hat	hat	has
.29	bikestool	Beichtstuhl	confessional
.30	fleshskin	Fläschchen	little flask
.32	sindbook	Sündenbock	scapegoat

.33	heldin	Heldin	heroine
230.8	mustered	Muster	pattern
.10	schortest	schor	sheared
.13	tosend	tausend	thousand
		tosend	raging, roaring
.14	Mondamoiseau	Mond	moon
.21	fingon	fing an	began
		fing	caught
.21	fluter	Flut	flood
.33	germane	Germane	Teuton
231.3	itch	ich	I
.13	freytherem	frey (archaic sp.)	free
.27	So is richt	So ist es recht	that is good or
		or richtig	right
.29	oldsteinsong	Stein	stone
.33	Ratskillers	Ratskeller	Town Hall cellar
232.2	mauwe	Möwe	seagull
.6	gang	Gang	walk, gait
.6	canty	Kante	edge; heel of bread
			loaf
.10	herzian	Herz	heart
.11	stell	stell-	to place
		Stelle	position, place
.23	lade!	lade!	load!
.32	Atlangthis	lang	long
.33	doubledasguesched	das	the
		Esche	ashtree
233.21	jaoneofergs	Ferge	ferryman
.27	Gau	Gau	district, province
.31	segur	Sieger	victor
.33	engelsk	Engel	angels
.34	raskly	rasch	quick
.35	spanich	nich'	not
		ich	I
234.2	sperrits	sperr-	close, barricade
.4	bruddy	Bruder	brother
.6	anybroddy	Bruder	brother
.7	kerl	Kerl	man, fellow

.9	breiches	Brei	mush
		Ei	egg
		Eiche	oak
.15	soulnetzer	Netz	net
		netzen	moisten
.18	suessiest	suess	sweet
.19	lusspillerindernees	Lustspiel	comedy
		Rinder	cattle
.28	safras durst assune	fraß	devoured
		Durst	thirst
		Sühne	atonement
.29	imbetther	im Bett	in the bed
.33	argan	arg	bad
235.1	salat	Salat	lettuce
.1	madiens'	dien-	serve
		Mädchen	girl
.4	blossful	bloß	naked
.5	farbung	Farbe	color
		Färbung	tint, dye
.28	uns	uns	us
.29	cousin gourmand	(German cousin)	
.35	hose	Hose	pants
236.4	bugling	bügeln	ironing
.5	sticksword	Stichwort	slogan; catch-word
.9	her and hin	hin und her	hither and thither
.9,10	paaralone	Paar	pair
.11	notes	Noten	music
.12 f	wibfrufrocksfull	Weib	woman, wife
		Fru (dial.)	woman, wife
.14	coo	Kuh	cow
.19	Rehmoose	Reh	deer
.24	platauplain	Tau	dew
.29	stimmering	Stimme	voice
.30	po's	Po	buttocks
.33	nattes	Natter	viper, adder
237.2	alls	als	as
.7	leichtly	leicht	easy, light
.7	see	sie	she
.12	aboutobloss	bloß	bare
.12	salutamt	Amt	office

.16	gab borab	gab	gave
		Rabe	raven
.19	oberblaseed	Ober	head waiter
			over
		Blase	blow, bubble
.20	hast	hast	(you) have
.29	youngling	Jüngling	youth
.31	Siker	sicher	sure
238.17	bisifings	beseifen	to soap
		bis	until
		fing	caught
.19	We ernst	wie ernst	how seriously
.22	mus	muß	must, necessity
.24	Herzog	Herzog	duke
.25	coosine	Kusine	female cousin
.26	Bohnaparts	Bohne	bean
		bohner	to polish, wax
.35	Daurdour	Dauer	duration, to last
239.7	Monkmesserag	Messer	knife
		Messe	mass
.10	Behose	Hose	pants
.12 f	hoaxites	Hochzeit	wedding
.13	gifting	Gift	poison
.16	Hightime	(lit.) Hochzeit	wedding
.17	fett	fett	fat
.18	Klitty	klittig	blotted, blurred
.18	scolderymeid	meid-	avoid
		Eid	oath
.19	stimm her uprecht	Stimme	voice, vote
		Stimmrecht	suffrage
		stimm-	tune (her upright piano)
		Ruprecht	Christian name
		aufrecht	upright
.23	bigyttens	begehen	to sin
.26	Whyfor	wofür	for which reason
.33	hellabelow	hell	bright
.35	broched	Broche	Hebrew prayer
240.2	wonna	Wonne	delight
.6	Examen	Examen	examination

.12	maden	Maden	maggots
.13	bletchendmacht	Blättchen	leaflet, membrane
		Macht	might, power
.16	rossum	Roß	steed
.18	Zundas	Zunder	tinder, fuse
.21	Calembaurnus	Bau	building
		Bauer	farmer
.24	Teufleuf	Teufel	devil
		tauf-	baptize
		Auflauf	soufflé
.25	mussymussy	Muß	must; necessity
.26	wolkenic	Wolken	clouds
.28	procent	Prozent	per cent
.34	ast	Ast	branch
.35	herrgott	Herrgott	Lord God
.35	tile	Teil	part
241.1	dumm crumm	dumm	dumb
		krumm	crooked
.1	akter	Akt	act, document; life model
.3	zuckers	Zucker	sugar
.7	house torts	Haustorte	term for unspecified kind of cake served by restaurant
.8	wert	wert	worth
.9 f	indicks weg	dick	thick, fat
		Weg	way
		weg	away
.10	funts	Fant	coxcomb
.14	Mereshame	Meerschaum	meershaum (sea foam)
.15	Aasdocktor	Aas	carrion
		Doktor	doctor
.16	mish	misch-	mix
.16	seinsed	sein	to be, his
		seins	his
.18	Meistral	Meister	master
		meist	most

.18 f	Noordwogen's kampften	Norwegen	Norway
		Wogen	waves
		kämpften	fought
.20	farrer	Pfarrer	priest
.21	prima	prima	excellent
.22	Milchku	Milchkuh	milk cow
.24	lochkneeghed forsunkener	Loch	hole
		Versunkener	one who has sunk
.24	stockknob	Stock	stick
.31	Ur	ur	primitive, first
		Uhr	clock
242.1	Heer	Heer	army
		Herr	Mr.
.2	den	den	that one
.2	laxtleap	Lachs	salmon
		lieb	dear
		Axt	axe
.5	nummer	Nummer	number
.5 f	wokinbetts	Wochenbett	childbed
.10	up excited	(lit.) aufgeregt	excited
.13	glycorawman	gleich	like
.15	wokklebout	wackel-	shake
.16	biss	biß	bit
		bis	until
.19	altfrumpishly	alt	old
.20	falls	falls	if, in case
.33	eckcot	Ecke	corner
.34	alleance	alle	all, everyone
243.1	yahrds	Jahr	year
.4	fiertey	vier	four
		vierte	fourth
.6	Schi schi	Schi	ski
.6	feightened	feig	cowardly
.8	pur	pur	pure
.10	feme	Feme	secret criminal court
.11	ruhm	Ruhm	fame
.16	sieme	sie	she

.16	roumanschy	Mansch	mixture; squash
		Mensch	person
.20	Winden wanden	winden	reel, twist
		wanden	reeled, twisted; turned
.20	wenden	wenden	turn
		wen denn	whom then
.23	nettleses	nett	nice
.26 f	Ostmannstown	Ostmann	East-man
.31	Rabbinsohn	Rab-	raven
		Rabbiner	rabbi
		Sohn	son
.36	widders	Widder	ram
244.13	tint	Tinte	ink
.16	frieren	frieren	freeze
.17	Zoo koud	zu kalt	too cold
.22	Far wol	Fahr wohl	drive (travel) well
.25	Lang	lang	long
.32	sheutseuyes	scheut	avoids, is shy of
.33	nicht	nicht	not
.34	leabarrow	lieb	dear
.34	loevdom	Löwe	lion
.35	Elenfant	Elefant	elephant
		Fant	coxcomb
.36	behemuth	Mut	courage
245.2	Hopopodorme	Popo	buttocks
.2 f	Sobeast	so bist	so (you) are
.7	mohns	Mohn	poppy
.7	bluming	Blume	flower
.8	siemens	sie	she, you
		Siemens	(electric appliances firm)
.14	horker	horche	listen
.15	munt	Mund	mouth
.16	Es	es	it; E-flat
.17	ges	geh-	go
		ges	G-flat
.18	Rosimund's	Mund	mouth
.22	Stright	Streit	quarrel

.23	forsehn	vorsehen	foresee
		sehn-	yearn
		Versehen	blunder
.23	wand	Wand	wall
.24	wenderer	wenden	turn
.26	mulligrubs	Müll	garbage
		Müllgrube	cesspit
.29	matt	matt	exhausted
.30	johl	johl-	hoot
.33	alefru's	Fru (dial.)	wife
246.4	felled	Feld	field
.6 f	Brandenborgenthor	Brandenburgertor	Brandenburg Gate (Berlin)
		borgen	borrow
.15	wonner	Wonne	delight
.15	ein	ein	one
.27	bartrossers	Bart	beard
		Roß	steed
.33	Bettlimbraves	Bett	bed
		betteln	beg
		brav im Bettli	well behaved in bed
247.1	taal	Tal	valley
.3	knychts	Knecht	servant
		nicht	not
.4	stucks	Stück	piece
		Stuck	plaster, stucco
.5	awage	Wage	scales
.6	lasterhalft	lasterhaft	vicious
		Laster	vice
		half	helped
.7	yougendtougend	Jugend	youth
		Tugend	virtue
.10	Barto	Bart	beard
.17	indeiterum	Eiter	pus
.20	ross	Roß	steed
.21	heaviered	vier	four
.22	eyerim	Eier	eggs
.23	Soldwoter	Sold	salary, reward
.27	maenneritsch	Männer	men
.29	warred	ward	became

.30	forebanned	verbannt	exiled
.31	heil	heil	hail
.35	feldgrau	feldgrau	fieldgray
248.6	unsatt speagle eye	unsatt	unsatisfied
		Spiegel	mirror
		Spiegelei	fried egg
.7	asters	Ast	branch
.13	solly	soll	should
		(Swiss pron. for)	(greeting)
		salut	
.13 f	pilger's fahrt	Pilgerfahrt	pilgrimage
.14	henker's	Henker	hangman
.15	halunkenend	Halunken	scoundrels
.17	Flo	Floh	flea
.22	Dunckle	dunkel	dark
.23	thicketloch	Loch	hole
.29	sprig	sprich	speak
.34	callby	Kalb	calf
.35	Radouga, Rab	Rad	wheel
		Rabe	raven
249.2	infuxes	Fuchs	fox
.7	rubinen	Rubinen	rubies
.7	elfinbone	Elfenbein	ivory
.9	therebeneath	(lit.) darunter	under it
.14	reder	Rede	speech
		Reeder	ship-owner
.17	augur	Auge	eye
.20	Oh backed von	Obacht vor dem	Look out for the
	dem zug!	Zug!	train!
.20	weg	Weg	way
.22	saum	Saum	hem, margin
.34	helf	helf-	help
.34	shauted	schaut	look
.35	hims prich	sprich	speak
.36	bloomers	Blume	flower
.36	gegging	gegen	against
250.3	Willest	willst	want
.3	rossy	Roß	steed

.4	rumpffkorpff	(echoes) Dumm-kopf	blockhead
		Rumpf	rump
		Kopf	head
.5	Swarthants	Schwarzer Hans	(devil-figure; a spirit of the fountain in a Grimm fairytale)
.5	shorn stile	Schornstein	chimney
.7	fro' Scheidam	scheiden	divorce, separate
		entscheiden	tell one from another; decide
.8	finges	fing (an)	started
.10	Spickspuk	spick-	smoke (meat)
		spuck	spit
		spuk	haunt
.11 f	Side here roohish, cleany fuglers!	Seid Ihr ruhig, kleine Vögel!	Hush, little birds!
.13	tantoncle's	Tante	aunt
		Onkel	uncle
.14	Yet's	jetzt	now
.17	moidered's lieb	Meuter-	mutiny
		lieb	dear
		Liebe	love
.17	herefore	hierfür	for this
.19	liebermann	lieber Mann	dear husband
.20	Liber	lieber	dear
.21	Link	links	left (direction)
.21	Leapermann	lieber Mann	dear husband
.24	rand	Rand	edge
.27	Nebnos	neben	next to
.27	Rosocale	Rosenkohl	cauliflower
.29	prunktqueen	Prunk	pomp
.31	vestin	Westen	shirts
			West
.34	ach	ach	oh
.35	farbetween	Farbe	color
251.7	spoors	Spur	trace
		spürt	senses
.10	stehs	steht	stands

251.15 f	viceheid	Weisheit	wisdom
		weiß	white
		heiß	hot
		Heide	heathen
.16	specks	Speck	bacon
.17	wishmarks	wisch-	wipe
.22	lerningstoel	lern-	learn
		Lehnstuhl	easy-chair
.36	gemurrmal	Gemurmel	murmuring
252.1	queering	queren	traverse
.1	shoolthers	Schulter	shoulder
.2	fausties	Faust	fist
.5	manchind's	manch-	some
.7	Mowy	Möwe	gull
.9	Feeling dank	vielen Dank	many thanks
.16	obscindgemeinded	gemein	mean
		Gemeinde	community
.23	richtly	richt-	judge, set right
.24	gar	gar	finished, cooked
.26	waterstichystuff	stich	sting
		Wasserstoff	hydrogen
		Stickstoff	nitrogen
253.4	mouthart	(lit.) Mundart	idiom
.5	mappamund	Mund	mouth
.17	garner	Garn	snare, decoy; yarn
.29	recken	recken	stretch
.31 f	childergarten	Garten	garden
.32	Lucanhof	Hof	court
254.3	Meereschal	Meeres Schale	bowl of the sea
.13	lauphed	lauf-	run
.13	minnelisp	Minne	love
.20	feel	viel	much
.21	furrinarr	Narr	fool
.25	Odam	Odem	breath
.28	Merodach	Dach	roof
.30	hut	Hut	hat
.30	hissarlik	häßlich	ugly
.31	hennin's	Hennen	hens
.33	sanger	Sänger	singer
255.8	webgoods	(lit.) Webwaren	textiles

.23	winkel	Winkel	angle, nook
256.1	eher	eher	before
.7	harns	Harn	urine
.7	Bier	Bier	beer
.7	Spirituosen	Spirituosen	liquor
.11	oddmund	Mund	mouth
.12	kindalled	Kind	child
		alt	old
.14	sterneward	Sterne	stars
		Sternwarte	observatory
.29	zentrum	Zentrum	centre
.30	radients	Rad	wheel
		dient	serves
.31 f	dinggyings	Ding	thing
.33	nibulissa	Nebel	fog
.34	alps on his druck-house	Druck	print
		Alpdruck	nightmare
257.1	bin	bin	am
.11	plattonem	platt	plain, vulgar
.19	weg	Weg	way
.21	Achin	ach	oh
.26	diesparation	dies	this
.28	abort . . . ort . . .	Abort	privy
		Ort	place
.29	Byfall	Beifall	applause
.31	schouwburgst	schau	look
		Burg	castle
258.1	Rendningrocks	Rock	skirt
.2	gttrdmmrng	Götterdämmerung	twilight of the gods
.3	Mannagad	Mann	man
.3	lammalelouh	Lamm	lamb
.4	fert	fertig	finished
.21	tambaldam	bald	soon
.21	tombaldoom	bald	soon
.24	tweedledeedumms	dumm	stupid
259.3 f	unlitten	litten	suffered
.10	Mummum	Mumm	courage
260.3	00	00	sign for toilet
.11	Brache	bräche	break

.12	querfixing	quer	across
.15	fahr	fahr	ride
.18	cuckling	Küchlein	chicken
261.2	petsybluse indecked	Bluse	blouse
		entdeckt	discovered
		Decke	cover
.3	elv	elf	eleven
.6 f	seakale	Siegel	seal
.7	befinding	befinden	find, consider
.13	*Tod*	Tod	death
.16	Glattstoneburg	glatt	smooth
		Burg	castle
.16	donnery	Donner	thunder
.25	mehrkurios	mehr	more
.25	saltz	Salz	salt
.31	decans	Dekan	dean
262.12	furscht kracht	Furcht	fear
		kracht	crashes
.15	Erdnacrusha	Erd-	earth
.22	skimmelk	melk-	to milk
		Schimmel	white horse
.23	over all	(lit.) überall	everywhere
.26 f	Inn inn! Inn inn!	Inn	(river)
.28	drang	drang	crowded
.31	Gotahelv	Gott	God
		helf	help
		Gotthelf	(Swiss novelist)
.32	er	er	he
.36	Achinhead	ach	oh
263.2	erst	erst	first
.11 f	postwartem	warten	wait
.15	Ganger	(Fuss)gänger	walker
.18	Saaleddies er	Saal	room
		er	he
.19	werden, mine	werden	will be
		mein	my
.20	alter	Alter	age
.35	Punt	Punkt	period
264.3	ernst	ernst	earnest

.6 f	backfrish	Backfisch	teen-ager
		frisch	fresh
.12 f	Ulma	Ulme	elm
.17	browses	Brause	shower
.27	ashwald	Wald	forest
265.2	Kloster	Kloster	cloister
.3 f	foregone on	(lit.) Voran-	the dead
		gegangene	
		vergangen	past, gone
.7	selfreizing	reiz-	attract; irritate
.10	niedelig	niedlich	pretty
		niedrig	low
.16	wonnerful	Wonne	delight
.27	wustworts	Wurst	sausage
		Wüste	desert
		Wort	word
266.5	toll	toll	mad
.8	Schein	Schein	shining, seeming
		schön	good, pretty
.8	Schore	schore	prop, support
.13	upsturts	Sturz	fall, overthrow
.15	nag	nag-	gnaw
.18	doll	doll, toll	extreme, mad
.20	Preausteric	Auster	oyster
.23	bancorot	bankrott	bankrupt
.24 f	catalaunic	Laune	mood, whim
.30	ondrawer	(lit.) Aufzieher	educator, tutor
.31 f	unterdrugged	unterdrückt	suppressed
267.3	maymeaminning of	Minne	love
	maimoomeining		
		Meinung	opinion
		Mai	May
.4	speer	Speer	spear
.8 f	endspeaking	(lit.) entsprechend	corresponding
.10	briefest	Brief	letter
.11	*Cis*	Cis	C sharp
.12	beckon	Becken	pelvis, bowl
.13	widerurges	wider-	against
		wieder	again
.17	selfloud	(lit.) Selbstlaut	vowel

.20	Weib	Weib	woman, wife
.20	Uwayoei	O Wehoweh!	Oh dear!
		Ei	egg
.20	mag	mag	may
.28	mistmusk	Mist	garbage
.29	meiblume	Maiblume	mayflower
268.2	enlocked	anlock-	beckon, seduce, allure
.11	grooser's	Gruß	greeting
		größer	greater
.12	grossopper's	groß	great
.22	oblative	Oblate	wafer
.26	Bott's trousend	Potz tausend!	(expletive)
.27	hore a man uff!	(dial.) hor emal uff!	stop it!
		(hör einmal auf!)	
.28	lewdy	Leute	people
.32	jungerl	jung	young
		Jünger	disciple
.35	Frech	frech	impudent
.36	Locklaun	lock-	beckon
		Laune	mood
269.3	dunk	dunkel	dark
.5	plaudered	plauder	gossip
.10	gerandiums	Rand	edge
.12	warthog	wart-	wait
.20	Werbungsap	Werbung	solicitation, wooing, advertising
.24	mauler	Maul	mouth, muzzle
.30	braught	Brau	brew
		Braut	bride
270.5	sollicitor's	soll	should
.7 f	lebbensquatsch	Leben	life
		Quatsch	nonsense
.10	waxedup	(lit.) aufgewachsen	grown up
.15	schlangder	Schlange	snake
		der	he
.26	muters	Mut	courage
		Mutter	mother

.27	Verschwindibus	verschwind	disappear
		verschwindibus	hocus pocus
.28	nimm	nimm	take
.28	nehm	nehm-	take
.30	ya, ya	ja	yes
.34	Lang Wang Wurm	lang	long
		Wange	cheek
		Wurm	worm
271.3	da, da	da	there
.5	hosies	Hose	pants
.18	gossans	goß	poured
		Gassen	streets
.19	Heber	Heber	lever, lifter, siphon
.24	earthapples	(lit.) Erdäpfel	potatoes
272.1	fromm	fromm	pious
.1	globing	glauben	believe
.2	hinder	hinter	behind
.5 f	warwhetswut	Wut	anger
.16 f	Blitzenkopfs	blitzen	lightning
		Kopf	head
.17	Hengegst	gegen	against
		Hengst	stallion
.25	Messherrn	Herrn	gentleman
		Messe	mass
		Messer	knife
.25	Brock	Brocken	crumb
.35	stimmstammer	Stimme	voice; vote
		stimm-	to be right
		Stamm	stem
273.3	bosthoon	Huhn	chicken
.4	Heil	heil	hail
.6	Fas est dass	Was ist das	what is that
.6	foe	wo	where
.12	nievre	nie	never
.19 f	freespeech	Freispruch	acquittal, absolution
.20	tep	Tepp, Depp	stupid person
.20	gar	gar	even, cooked
.20 f	hintergrunting	Hintergrund	background
.22	laubhing	Laub	foliage
		hing	hung

.25	winker	Winker	signal; flagman
.28	hoerse	hör-	listen
.31	Huhneye	Huhn	chicken
		(lit.) Hühnerauge	corn (on the foot)
274.1	emblem	blem	dumb, eccentric
.2	*Murdoch*	doch	yet
.14	speel	spiel-	play
.17	elfshot	elf	eleven
.23	puta	Pute	hen
.25	windstill	Windstille	calm
275.8	Standfest	stand fest	stood fast
		standfest	steadfast
.14	Blowyhart	hart	hard
276.5	blost	bloß	naked
.6	*pulfers*	Pulver	powder
.9 f	Ough, ough, brieve	Auch, auch, brav'	that too, good little
	kindli	Kindli	child
.13	Zumbock!	Zum Bock!	The devil!
			(lit.: to the goat)
.14	fadervor	(lit.) Vorvater	ancestor
.16	lecking	leck-	lick, leak
.20	flou	flau	feeble, lukewarm,
			slack
277.4	*spick*	spick-	smoked (of meat)
.15	*Gautamed*	Gau	county
.18	Sein	sein	being
.20	herbest	Herbst	autumn
		herb	austere
278.7	Bewise	Beweise	proofs
.9	lets to hear	(lit.) läßt zu hören	expresses himself
.17	*Brotus*	Brot	bread
.32	pohlmann's	Mann	man
.38	weggin	wegen	because of
		(Sw.) Weggen	breadroll
279.2	cult	kalt	cold
.3	yore	Jahr	year
.14	sh'undn't	Schund	trash
		und	and
.18	toloseher	Seher	seer
.22	seidens	Seiden	silks

.24	fuchsia	Fuchs	fox
.26	spickness	spick-	smoked (of meat)
.31	reized	reiz	attract; irritate
.33	Bina de Bisse	beinah	almost
		Biß	bite
.33	von	von	of
.34	Sago	sag-	say
		Sage	saga
.39	mench	Mensch	person
280.13	*shieling*	schiel	squint
281.11	*Also Spuke*	Also sprach	Thus spoke
		Spucke	spit
		spuk	haunt
.21	aerger	Ärger	anger
.23	Sieger	Sieger	victor
.23	Ruhm	Ruhm	fame
.26	ruck	Ruck	jolt, move
.26	Enten	Enten	ducks
.33	nateswipe	nett's Weib	nice girl, woman
.33	pulper	Pulver	powder
282.7	flink	flink	quick
.7	freck	frech	fresh, impudent
.7	stern	Stern	star
.9	bekase	Käse	cheese
.22	weisswassh	weiß	white
		weiß was	know what
283.1	Enoch Thortig	noch	yet
		-ig	(Gm. suffix)
.7	loaferst	erst	first
.8	sexes	sechs	six
.13	links	links	left
.14	tods	Tod	death
.19	*Dondderwedder*	Donnerwetter	(expletive)
.20	*Kyboshicksal*	keibe	(expletive)
		Schicksal	fate
.22	rede	rede	speak
.28 f	herman dororrhea	Hermann und	(Goethe narrative
		Dorothea	poem)
.29	fantods	Tod	death
.31	kinder	Kinder	children

.10	glike	gleich	like, equals
.12	minney	Minne	love
.14	rute	Rute	rod, switch
.23	bissyclitties	Biß	bite
.26	upsittuponable	Sitte	custom
		(lit.) aufsässig	refractory
.31	Dudeney	Duden	(lexicographer)
.31	putch	Putsch	revolutionary
			outbreak
285.1	lenz	Lenz	spring
.1	habby	habe	have
		Habe	possession
.2	erdor	Erde	earth
.4	hare and dart	hier und dort	here and there
.10	himmulteemiously	Himmel	heaven, sky
.11	ersed ladest mand	erst	first
		ladest	(you) invite
		Mand	moon, month
.12	uhu	Uhu	owl
.19	seitseman	seit	since
.29 f	prostalutes	prost	bless you, cheers
.32	rossies	Rosse	steeds
286.7	nettus	nettes	nice
.14	radmachrees	Rad	wheel
.14	rossecullinans	Roß	steed
.18	fort	fort	away
.19	ferst	erst	first
.20	Probe	Probe	trial, rehearsal
.22	*browd*	Braut	bride
.36	sugans	Gans	goose
287.2 f	ganswer	Gans	goose
		wer	who
.5	mut	Mut	courage
.6	bach	Bach	spring, brook
.12	Gu it	gut	good
.13	Mux	mach's	make it, do it
		mag's	may
.19	gert	Gerte	twitch, switch
.19	stoan	Stöan	stone (Austr. dial.)
.19	balbose	böse	naughty, evil

.31	piz . . .	Piz	peak, Mount . . .
288.2	mottes	Motte	moth
.9	faust	Faust	fist
.12	hexenshoes	Hexen	witches
		Hexenschuß	lumbago
.17	P. T. Publikums	P. T.	(Gm. abbr. for *praemissis titulis* [omitting the usual titles], often found on public notices, theater programs, and the like)
		Publikum	the public
.26	bloot	Blut	blood
.26	braim	Bräme	brim
.26	brile	Brei	porridge
		Brille	spectacles
.33	creek and veek	Krieg	war
		krieg'	get
		wieg'	weigh
.35	. . . mond . . .	Mond	moon
289.9	Derzherr	Der Erzherzog	the Archduke
		Herr	Lord
.10	Funkling	Funk-	spark
.11 f	underlacking	Unterlack	primer coat
		Laken	sheet
.18	gang	Gang	going
.19	schlang	Schlange	snake
.20	magdies	Magd	maid
290.8	lauschening	lauschen	listen
.12 f	Blinkensope's	Blinken	sparkle
.15	fearfeel	verfiel	disintegrated
.17	wush	wusch	washed
.18	Fogloot	Glut	glow
.22	lampblick	Blick	look, view
.25	spottprice	spott-	sarcastic, laughable
		Spottpreis	a ridiculously low price

.27	firma	Firma	company
.28	craft	Kraft	power, strength
.36	bookley	Buckel	hump
291.1 f	cornwer	wer	who
.9	hut	Hut	hat
.12	juwelietry	Juwel	jewel
.19	Papesthorpe	Papst	pope
.22	amarm	umarm	embrace
.22	miching	mich	me
.23	micher's	mich	me
.23	gaulish	Gaul	horse
.32	stern	Stern	star
292.22	crame	Kram	rubbish
.22	faustian	Faust	fist
.23	launer's lightsome	Laune	mood
		Leichtsinn	frivolity
.23	schwearmood	Schwermut	melancholy
.27	landsmaul	Maul	mouth, muzzle
.27	half	half	helped
.27	helf	helf	help
.27	holf	-holf-	helped
.27	salb	Salbe	salve
.30	sternly	Stern	star
.34	brut	Brut	brood
293.1	Cossist	Was ist?	what's wrong?
.22	Von	von	of
.23	ding	Ding	thing
.24	Ulm	Ulme	elm
		Ulm	(city, Einstein's birthplace)
.34	Draumcondra's	Traum	dream
.35	toadhauntered	Tod	death
294.8	*Sarga*	Sarg	coffin
.10	Allow ter	lauter	louder; pure
.14	entducked	entdeckt	discovered
		Ente	duck
.18	boudeville	Bude	hut
.19	raucking	rauch	smoke
.20	smukking	Schmuck	decoration, jewelry

.21	seesidling	Siedlung	settlement, housing tract
.31	quer	quer	across
295.1 f	istherdie	ist	is
.18	nothung	Nothung	(Siegfried's sword)
.26	nesse	Nässe	wetness
.26	nace	naß	wet
.27	allus	alles	everything
.28	kunst	Kunst	art
.34	beillybursts	Beil	hatchet
.35	Kelleiney	Keller	cellar
		Leine	leash, rope
		Kelle	trowel
296.1	Nun	nun	now
.2	quatsch	Quatsch	nonsense
.3	punctum	Punkt	period
.6	Hoddum	Hode	testicle
.8	*Zweispaltung*	Zweispaltung	bifurcation
.10 f	*Wiederherstellung*	Wiederherstellung	reconstitution
.22	pfan	Pfanne	pan
297.3	seel	Seele	soul
.3 f	hexengown	Hexen	witches
.13	winkles	Winkel	angle
.15	Lob	lob	praise
.31	rutches	rutsch-	slide
.32	Afrantic	Aff'	ape
.32	bett und bier	Bett	bed
		und	and
		Bier	beer
.34	egal	egal	equal
.36	meinkind	mein Kind	my child
298.4	riffa	Riff	reef
.9	Doll	toll	mad, extreme
.11	Doll	toll	mad, extreme
.17	fickers	fick-	move quickly to and fro, cohabit
.28 f	perimutter	Perlmutter	mother of pearl
.31	manier and manier	Manier	manner
299.1	scherts	Scherz	joke
.2	ichs	ich	I

.2	euchs	Euch	to you
.3	feared	vier	four
.9	Krumwall	krumm	crooked
.10	ueber	über	over
.14	gheist	Geist	ghost
		heißt	is called
.16	loiternan's	Laterne	lantern
		Leute	people
.22 f	Hammeltones	Hammel	wether, sheep
.29	lauffe	laufe	run
300.5	wanigel	Igel	hedgehog
.15	fress up	freß auf	gobble
.16	rinnerung	Erinnerung	memory
		Rinne	gutter, trough
.21	deleberate	Leber	liver
.24	mund	Mund	mouth
.25	grafficking	Graf	earl
		fick-	cohabit
.31 f	*No Sturm.*	Sturm	storm
	No Drang.	Drang	violence
		Sturm und Drang	Storm and Stress (literary movement)
301.2	Es war	Es war	it was
.5	bosthoon	Huhn	chicken
.18	steifel	steif	stiff
		Stiefel	boots
.23	plankraft	Kraft	power, strength
.26	diesmal	diesmal	this time
302.4	Punked	Punkt	period, stop
.21	Ohr	Ohr	ear
.22	olchedolche	Dolche	daggers
.22	lunge	Lunge	lung
.26	Unds	und	and
		uns	us
.28	Outstamp	(German method of forming verb)	
.33	knacking	knack-	crack
303.20	hof	Hof	court
.23	pergaman	Pergament	parchment

.26	firstings	Fürsten	dukes
.33	speel	spiel	play
304.3	Formalisa	Mild und leise	(love-death aria)
.9	rayingbogeys	Regenbogen	rain-bow
.9	rings round me	(lit.) rings rum	all round
.12	funfer	Fünfer	five-penny coin
.20	she studiert whas	sie studiert, was?	she studies, eh?
.28	ambows	Amboß	anvil
305.6	Eyeinstye	Einstein	(physicist)
		einst	once
.10 f	wortsampler	Wort	word
.19 f	Biddy's hair. Biddy's hair, mine lubber	Bitte sehr, mein Lieber	You're welcome, dear
.24	Bide in	beiden	to both
.25	Bide in	beiden	to both
.29	steyne	Stein	stone
.31	lobe	Lob	praise
306.2	neckkandcropfs	Kropf	craw
		neckend	teasing
.3	Heavysciusgardaddy	gar	even, cooked
.4	gift uns	Gift	poison
		uns	us
.35	Bubabipibambuli	Bub	boy
307.34	Mich	mich	me
308.15	Kakao-	Kakao	cocoa
.33	anticheirst	ich	I
		erst	first
309.4	stammpunct	Standpunkt	standpoint
		Stamm	origin; stem
.24	marygoraumd	Raum	room, space
310.3 f	Jomsborg	borg	borrow
.4	Selverbergen	bergen	dig up; hide
.8	serostaatarean	Staat	the State
.16	Olegsonder	Sonder-	special
.16	-Rosses	Roß	steed
.17	Rhosso-	Roß	steed
.17	Zastwoking	wo	where
.19	buckling	Buckel	hump
		Bückling	kipper
.19	hummer	Hummer	lobster

.22	cartomance	Karte	map
.24	Nur	nur	only
.24	immerges	immer	always
.28	luckybock	Bock	he-goat
.30	teller	Teller	plate, dish
311.4	theygottheres	Gott	God
.6	ohr	Ohr	ear
.9	Norweeger's	Norweger	a Norwegian
.11	wickser	Wichse	thrashing
		Wichser	bootblack, guttersnipe
.21	sagd	sagt	says
.24	tayleren	lehren	teach
.33	fur	für	for
312.1	Stolp, tief, stolp	stolpern	stumble
		tief	deep
.6	sailend sonnen-rounders	elend	miserable
		Sonnen	suns, of the sun
.12	raign	Regen	rain
.13	broaders-	Brüder	brothers
.16	Nett sew?	nett	nice
		nicht so?	isn't that so?
.19	whol niet	(dial.) wohl nit (wohl nicht)	surely not
.25	wohl yeas	wohl ja	surely yes
313.4	Sets on sayfohrt	setz an sofort	start immediately
		Fahrt	trip
.20	ast	Ast	branch
.25	mine	mein	my
.25	juwels	Juwel	jewel
.25	Nummers	Nummer	number
.34	towerds	Erde	earth
		werd-	become
.35	hodden	Hoden	testicles
.35	pookal	Pokal	wine-cup
314.1	deiffel	Teufel	devil
.12	Rutsch	rutsch-	slide
.18	hoch	hoch	high; hail
.18	lach	lach-	laugh
.20	lauf	lauf-	run; gun barrel

.21	Paradoxmutose	Mut	courage
.24	ringround	(lit.) ringsum	all around
.28	sohns	Sohn	son
.28	blitzh	Blitz	lightning
.31	ungkerls	Kerl	guy
.32	bouchal	Bauch	belly
.34	*ros*	Roß	steed
315.1	davors	davor	before that
.3	Knit wear?	Nicht wahr?	Isn't that so?
.13	reiter	Reiter	rider
.21	sagd	sagt	says
.22	bierhiven	Bier	beer
.23	weg	Weg	road
.24	horenpipe	hören	hear
.28	fand	fand	found
.31	langseling	langsam	slow
.35	lauwering	lau	lukewarm
		lauern	lurk
316.4	ast	Ast	branch
.8	heft	Heft	notebook
.13	Kinkincaraborg	borg-	borrow
.14	overlive	(lit.) überleben	survive
.17	doomering	Dämmerung	twilight
.18	sess	sess-	sit
.18	soss	Soße	sauce
.22	gang	Gang	going, gait
.27	bliakings	blick-	look
.28	furt	Furt	ford
.29	hurdies	Hürde	hurdle
.30	lurch	Lurch	amphibious animal
.33	sagd	sagt	says
.35	bit bite	(lit.) bißchen	little
.36	keesens	Kies	gravel
		Kissen	pillow
.36	sagd	sagt	says
317.1	sagd	sagt	says
.2	fro	froh	merry
.4	sagd ... sagd	sagt	says
.10	wilcomer	willkommen	welcome

.12	osturs	Ost	East
		Oster-	Easter
		stur	stubborn
.15	sonnur	Sonnenuhr	sun dial
		nur	only
.16	Opvarts	aufwärts	upward
		abwärts	downward
.19	meer crank	mehr	more
		Meer	sea
		krank	sick
.20	fare	Fähre	ferry
.21	wehrn	weh	woe
		wehren	defend
.26	mistaenk	Mist	garbage
		stänk-	stink; complain
.27	taler	Tal	valley
		Taler	(coin)
.34	haares	Haar	hair
318.9 f	youngfree	Jungfrau	maiden
.10	stilling	stillen	quench, nurse
.11	Annexandreian	drei	three
.12	Spaight	Specht	woodpecker
		spät	late
.14	han	Hahn	cock
.14	hende	Hände	hands
		Hendl (dial.)	chicken, hen
.22	aurowoch	Woche	week
.27	Womensch plodge	wo	where
		Mensch	person
		Platz	place, room
319.4	usquebauched	Bauch	belly
.9	Maut	Maut	excise, toll
		mau	middling
.21	fatter	Vater	father
.21	apopo	Popo	buttocks
.21	buckseaseilers	Büchse	box, trousers
		Seiler	ropemaker
		Eile	hurry
.23	sagd	sagt	says
.24	teller	Teller	plate

.26	marinned	rinnt	flows, trickles
.26	gargantast	gar	even
		Gant	auction
		antast-	touch
.27	Wolafs	wo	where
		wohl	well
		Aff'	ape
.27	sagd	sagt	says
.28	sigen	Segen	bless
		siegen	conquer
.29	carsed	Karst	mattock; chalky ground (f. i., near Trieste)
.30	Hops	hops	hola!; pregnant (sl.)
.30	sagd	sagt	says
.31	lauffed	läuft	runs
.35	debauchly	Bauch	belly
320.1	sagd	sagt	says
.1	enderer	Änderer	one who changes something
.2	sagd	sagt	says
.3	after inunder	(lit.) nacheinander	after each other
.4	stitchimesnider	Schneider	tailor
.5	budinholder	Bude	hut
.5	cummanisht	komme nicht	am not coming
.5, 6, 8	sagd	sagt	says
.9	hamd	Hemd	shirt
.9	tollerloon	toller	mad, fantastic
		Lohn	reward, wage
.9	sagd	sagt	says
.9	brofkost	Briefkasten	mail-box
		Kost	diet, food
		Rohkost	diet of uncooked food
.10	bangd	bangt	yearns for, fears
.11	sagd	sagt	says
.11	behunt	Hund	dog
		behend(e)	quick, nimble
.12	sagd	sagt	says

.13	mundering	Mund	mouth
.14	shimps names	schimpf-	scold
		Schimpfname	abusive name
.14	gitter	Gitter	grating, bars
.14	sagd	sagt	says
.19	hised	heißt	names, is called
.22	rund turs	rund	round, around
		Tür	door
.26 f	wackering	wacker	brave
		wackel	totter, stagger
.28	Afferik	Affe	ape
321.1	oelkenner	Öl	oil
		Kenner	expert, connoisseur
.4	lawstift	Stift	stylus; convent, foundation
.4	wand	Wand	wall
.11	kiber	Keibe	(expletive)
.12	Wazwollenzee Haven	Was wollen Sie haben	what do you want
.23	gaul	Gaul	horse, nag
.28	drohnings	droh-	threaten
		dröhnen	roar, resound
		Drohne	drone
.29	trink	trink	drink
322.3 f	so was	so was!	imagine!
.10	misfutthered	Futter	fodder; lining, sheath
		Futt (sl.)	vagina
.21	tassed	Tasse	cup
		tast-	touch, grope
.21	sassed	saß	sat
.21	tager	Tag	day
		tagen	hold a meeting
.25	horces	horch	listen
323.1	bummell	Bummel	stroll, promenade
.1	wanderducken	ducken	stoop, bow, duck
.9	Donnerbruch	Donner	thunder
		Bruch	break

(probably suggested by Wolkenbruch, a cloudburst)

.13	Meistr	meist	mostly
		Meister	master
.16	faus	Faust	fist
.19	zirkuvs	Zirkus	circus
.19	teilwrmans	teil	part
.21	Mecckrass	meckern	bleat
		Rasse	race
		kraß	crass
.26	ukonnen	können	can, are able
.34	cram bokk	Kram	rubbish
		Bock	he-goat
.36	gang	Gang	walk, gait
.36	dane and dare	den und der	this one and that one
.36	spuk	spuck-	spit
		spuk-	haunt
324.9	Thallasee	See	sea, lake
.13	Underbund	Bund	bunch, union
.13	overraskelled	überrascht	surprized
		Kelle	trowel
.16	allohn	Lohn	reward, wage
		ohn-	without
.21	Ellers	Eller	alder
.24	Welter	Welt	world
		Wetter	weather
.25	nordth	Nord	North
.28	muster	Muster	pattern, paragon
.36	abbroaching	ab-	off
		abbrechen	break off, break up
325.11, 12	christianismus	-nismus	-ism
.12	pellover	pell-	peel
.14	laun	Laune	mood, whim
.16	seelord	See	sea
		Seele	soul
.16	gosse	Gosse (Gasse)	gutter, alley
.26	blooders'	Bruder	brother
.31	wutan	Wut	anger
		wüten	to rage
.31	whaal	Wal	whale
		Wahl	choice

.32	Blass	blaß	pale
326.5	beheild	heil!	hail!
		heilt	heals
.5	ouishguss	Guß	gush, outpour
.8	furst	Fürst	prince
.8 f	gielgaulgalls	Giel (Swiss)	bay
		Gaul	horse, nag
.10	aase	Aas	carrion, carcass
.16	saelir	Seele	soul
.17	gott kvold	Gott	god
		quoll	oozed, sprung
.19	sael	Seele	soul
.20	Spickinusand	spicken	to smoke (meat)
.26	aaherra	Herr	master, gentleman
.30 f	eurekason	Eure	your (plural)
327.1	smukklers	Schmuck	jewelry
.1	forelooper	verloben	engage to marry
.10	saft	Saft	juice
		sacht	softly
.13	glatsch	glatt	smooth
		klatsch-	applaud
.15	stuffel	Stuffel	step, ladder rung
		Staffel	ladder rung, easel
.16	rossies	Roß	steed
.20	summwer	summ-	hum
		wer	who
.28	gift	Gift	poison
.33	Humpopolamos	Popo	posterior
.34	aasbukividdy	Aas	carrion
328.10	bach	Bach	brook
.10	donochs	dennoch	nevertheless
		noch	yet, in addition
.14	Sheeres	Schere	scissors
.16	herberge	Herberge	shelter, hostel
		Berge	mountains
.22	brottels	Brot	bread
		Rotte	troop, horde
.25	ringsengd ringsengd	seng-	singe
		eng	narrow
.25	Erho	er	he

.26	Referinn Fuchs	Rinne	gutter
		rinn-	run, flow
		Fuchs	fox
.26	Gutmann	gut	good
		Mann	man, husband
.26	*Welled*	Welt	world
329.7	Fuss	Fuß	foot
.8	Muss	muß	must
.9	anker	Anker	anchor
.10	chenchen	-chen	(diminutive suffix)
.11	bettest	Bett	bed
.19 f	hooneymoon	Huhn	hen
.28	owfally	auffall-	noticeable, remarkable
.29	Meckl	meck-	bleat
		Mecklenburg	(territory on Baltic)
.31	hafts	Haft	rivet, brace; hold
.33	Fathach	ach	oh
330.1	Suenders	Sünder	sinner
.5	Matt	matt	exhausted
.18	feines	Feines	something excellent
.18	sinns	Sinn	opinion, sense
.21	holder	hold	handsome
		Holder	friend; elderwood
.22	polder	Polder	reclaimed marshland
.23	scorenning	renn-	run, race
.23	Kitzy	Katze	cat
		Kitz	kitten, kid
.24	Kleinsuessmein	klein	small
		süß	sweet
		mein	mine
.28	wohl's	wohl	well, health
.36	moder of moders	Moder	mud, decay
331.10	durst	Durst	thirst
.16	grosskropper	groß	great
.18	kerls	Kerl	guy
.26	sommerlad	Sommer	summer
332.4	hanigen	Hahn	cock

.4	hunigen	Huhn	chicken
.5	hinnigen	hin	gone, ruined
		Henne	hen
.5 f	... lachnatullagh ...	lach-	laugh
		natürlich	naturally
.7	creeked	kriegt	gets
.15	gribgrobgrab	grob	coarse, rude
		Grab	grave; dug
.18	allamarsch	Marsch	march
.18	Kaemper Daemper	Kämpe	champion
		Kämpfe	fights, battles
		Dampfer	steamship
		Dämpfer	damper
.21	tondur	Ton	tone
		dur	major key
.22	leedy	Lied	song
.28	synnbildising	Sinnbild	symbol, emblem
		Sinn	sense
		Bild	picture, image
333.4	shoehandschiner	Handschuh	glove
		schein-	shine, appear
.8	danzing	Danzig	(city)
.11 f	upstored	(lit.) aufbewahrt	kept safe
.13	remoltked	von Moltke	(general)
.22	dronnings	drohen	threaten
		dröhnen	roar, resound
.22	beeswixed	Wichse	polish; spanking
.22	fang	fang	caught
.32	dursted	Durst	thirst
.34	obayre	Ober	waiter
		ob er	whether he
.34	Mattom	matt	exhausted, checkmate
.34	pfot	Pfot-	paw
.35	chach	Schach	chess; check!
		ach	oh
.36	morrienbaths	Marienbad	(town)
334.1	spick's	spick-	smoke (meat)
.3	Kostello	Kost	diet, food
.7	toll hut	toller Hut	mad hat

.18	prosit	Prosit!	To your health!
.21	jude	Jude	jew
.24	pobbel	Pöbel	rabble
.27	flundered	Flunder	flounder
.29	duft	Duft	aroma
.36	lipe	Leib	body
335.4	Au! Au! Aue!	Au!	oh! (ouch!)
		Aue!	oh! (ouch!);
			meadow
.4	Heish	heiß	hot
		Eis	ice
		heisch-	demand, command
.10	hundt	Hund	dog
.12	vastelend	Elend	misery
.12 f	hosteilend	Ost	East
		steil	steep
		eilend	hurrying
		teilend	dividing
.13	neuziel	neu	new
		Ziel	target, goal
.13	oltrigger	alt	old
.17	sturm	Sturm	storm
		Turm	tower
.18	maormaoring	Marmor	marble
.18	sturm	Sturm	storm
.18	waxes	wachse	grow
.18 f	fuercilier	für	for
		fürchterlich	terribly
.19	sturm	Sturm	storm
.23	Au! Au! Aue!	Au!	oh! (ouch!)
		Aue!	oh! (ouch!); .
			meadow
.23	Heish	heiß	hot
		Eis	ice
		heisch-	demand, command
.26	underthaner	Unterthan	vassal
		(arch. sp.)	
.27	sint	sind	are
.32	lang	lang	long
336.5	messer's	Messer	knife

.12	wasch	wasch	wash
.13	fhronehflord	frönen	toil, drudge
.21	gartener	Garten	garden
.28	welt	Welt	world
337.6	mleckman	meck-	bleat
		leck-	lick
.7	freudzay	Freude	joy
.9	lude	Lied	song
.11	dulled in	dulden	suffer, permit
.11	bleakhusen	liebkosen	caress
.16	wosen	Rosen	roses
.18	stotterer	Stotterer	stutterer
.19	tritt	tritt	step, stepped
.21	lobstarts	Lob	praise
.24	wollies	Wolle	wool
.28	pritt	ritt	rode
.34	rucks	rucks-	coo (of birds)
.34	Gereland	Gier	greed, lust
.34	bettlle	bettel	beg
		Bett	bed
338.3	Ehren	Ehren	honors
.5	*freers*	frier-	freeze
.8	*rhyttel*	rüttel	shake
.11	*mottledged*	Motte	moth
.12	*motto*	Motte	moth
.13	*da*	da	there
.16	bitly	bitte	please
		bißchen	a bit, a little
.17	unt	und	and
.18 f	side in	Seiden	silks
.19	gubernier-gerenal	Niere	kidney
.19	laut-lievtonant	laut	loud; sound
		Ton	tone
.20	langdwage	lang	long
		wage	dare
.21	Shelltoss	schelt-	scold
.22	welltass	Welt	world
		Tasse	cup
		aß	ate
.25	tammit	damit	with it

.27	Rassamble	Rasse	race
.32	bobbycop	Bubikopf	bobbed hair style
.34	*whereis*	Reis	rice
		Eis	ice
.35 f	*weitoheito langthorn*	weiter	onward
		heiter	merry
		lang	long
339.2	narar	Narr	fool
.2	sann	sann	meditated
.4	gut	gut	good
.5	fudden	Faden	thread
.5	pitschobed	schob	pushed
.5	metchennacht	Mädchen	girl
		Nacht	night
.6	belaburt	(Ge)burt	birth
.6	carsse	Karst	chalky ground
.6	gam	Gams	goat
.7	behund	Hund	dog
		behend	quick, nimble
.8	ros	Roß	steed
.8	bell	bell-	bark (dog)
.10	wappents	Wappen	insignia, crest
.10	raglanrock	Rock	jacket, skirt
.12	blousejagged	Jagd	hunt
.12	manchokuffs	manche	some
		Manschette	cuff
.14	beromst	berühmt	famous
		rühmst	praise
		Rom	Rome
.14	Karrs	Karre	cart
.18 f	*waggonhorchers*	Waggon	wagon
		horch-	listen
.21	*blickblackblobs*	blick-	look
		Lob	praise
.21	Grozarktic!	großartig!	magnificent!
.21	Toadlebens!	Tod	death
		Leben	life
.26	alleyou	alle	everyone
.31	*strick*	Strick	rope, halter
.35	*vatercan*	Vater	father

.36	*emt*	Amt	office
340.5	*mistomist*	Mist	garbage
.8	felled	Feld	field
.9	lomondations	Mond	moon
.11	aspoor	Spur	trace, track
.21	manmichal	man	one
		mich	to me
.22	fined	Feind	enemy
.24	Guards, serf	Gott strafe England	God punish
	Finnland		England
.32	soll	soll	should
.35	Riss	Riß	tear
.35	Ross	Roß	steed
341.4	*innermals*	-mals	-times
.4	*spool*	Spiel	game, play
.10	*hummer*	Hummer	lobster
.11	*fumfing*	fing	caught
.12	wartar	wart-	wait
.17	pife	Pfeife	pipe
.17	mlachy	lach-	laugh
.30	*kenneldar*	dar	there
.34	*blued*	Blut	blood
342.3	*deck*	deck-	cover, set
.6	*Baldawl*	bald	soon
.7	*shick*	schick-	send
.14	*Gross*	groß	great
.18	*hross*	Roß	steed
.19	*shote*	Schote	pod; dear old
			friend
.24	*Furstin*	Fürstin	princess
.29	*shinkly*	Schinken	ham
.30	*Bett*	Bett	bed
343.2	carsst	Karst	chalky ground
.5	armeemonds	Armee	army
		Mond	moon
.11	chooldrengs	dräng-	press, crowd
.18 f	*popoporportiums*	Popo	posterior
.20	Ichts	ich	I
.20	nichts on nichts	nichts	nothing
.21	schpirrt	irrt	is mistaken

.22	schkrepz	Krebs	cancer, crab
.22	qwehrmin	quer	across
		wehr-	defend
		Gewehr	rifle
		Wehrmann	soldier
.23	grandoper	Oper	opera
.25	duhans	du, Hans	you, Hans
.27	pulversporochs	Pulver	powder
		Spur	trace
		roch	smelled; smoked
.28	nemesisplotsch	nehmen Sie Platz	have a seat
		platsch!	splash!
.33	haftara	haft-	guarantee
		Haft	arrest, custody
.35	bibbering	beben	quake
		bibbern	tremble
		Biber	beaver
.35	vear	vier	four
.36	Flute	Flut	flood
344.1	*unglucksarsoon*	Unglück	bad luck, accident, misery
6.	Papaist	Papst	pope
		ist	is
.9	*strafe*	Strafe	punishment
.12	*bleyes*	Blei	lead
.14	nitshnykopfgoknob	nit (dial.)	not
		Kopf	head
		Knab'	boy, lad
.16	Messar	Messer	knife
.23	veereyed	vier	four
		wir	we
.28	gut	gut	good
.29	bubbering	Bub	boy
.30	tob tob tob	tob-	rage, play violently
.30	Clummensy	klommen	climbed
		kommen Sie!	come!
.34	arge	arg	bad, extreme
.35	rueckenased	Rücken	back
		Nasenrücken	bridge of the nose
.35	fear	vier	four

.1	hairmaierians	Herr Maier	Mr. Mayer
		Mai	May
.2	achaura	ach	oh
.4	*waldmanns*	Waldmann	forester
.8	Grot Zot	Grot	groat
		groß	great
		Zote	obscenity
.13	Merzmard	März	March
		merz-	reject
.24	Trink	trink	drink
.25	orafferteed	raff-	snatch
		Affe	ape
		fertig	finished
.26	*phot*	Pfote	paw
		Futt (sl.)	vagina
.28	*trosstpassers*	Troß	military baggage
		Trost	consolation
		Spaß	fun, joke
.32	foerses	Ferse	heel
.33	boesen fiennd	bösen	evil
		Feind	enemy
.35	*foregotthened*	Gott	god
.35	*abbosed*	ab	off
		böse	evil, angry
.36	*teilweisioned*	teilweis	partly
		weis-	wise
346.1	*affubling*	Affe	ape
.7	*jehumispheure*	Feuer	fire
		Eure	your (plural)
.15	*buckthurnstock*	turn-	do gymnastics
		Stock	stick
.18	*agamb ... agam*	Gams	goat
.23	offgott	Abgott	idol
.23	affsang	Affe	ape
.23	buthbach	Bach	brook
.30	sneezturmdrappen	Schneesturm	snowstorm
		Turm	tower
		Rappen	(Swiss coin); horse
.34	*allatwanst*	Wanst	belly
347.4	elve	elf	eleven

.6	blodidens	blöde	silly
.6 f	hegheg	heg-	protect, shelter
.7	wetter	Wetter	weather
.9	asundurst	Sünde	sin
		Durst	thirst
.9	Woolwichleagues	wich	dodged, yielded
.11	stillstumms	stumm	dumb, silent
.11	freshprosts	Prost!	To your health!
.13	wapping stiltstunts	Wappen	insignia
		Waffenstillstand	truce
.32	Crummwiliam	krumm	crooked
.34	*beheiss*	beheiz-	heat
		heiß	hot; be called
.35	*feuer*	Feuer	fire
.36	*smolking*	molk-	milked
.36	*rooking*	rauchen	smoking
348.5	rassociations	Rasse	race
8.	bleime	Blei	lead
		Leim	glue
.10	waulholler	Walhalla	(home of gods)
.11	dring	dring-	urge, press, throng
.13	wehrmuth	wehr-	defend
		Mut	courage
		Wehrmacht	army
.16	Neuilands	neu	new
.22	khakireinettes	rein	clean, pure
		nette	nice ones
.25	wamth	Wams	jacket
.25	lyse	leise	quiet
349.2	Ist	ist	is
.2	gonorrhal stab	Generalstab	general staff
.3	marsh	marsch	march
.4	dingbut	Ding	thing
.4	zahur and	Zar und Zimmer-	(opera:) Czar and
	zimmerminnes	mann	Carpenter
		Hure	prostitute
		Zimmer	room; (author)
		Minne	love
.12	*bitts*	Bitte	please
.15	*nichilite*	nicht	not

.17	*Shlossh*	Schluß	end
		Schloß	lock; castle
.17	*caeseine*	Käse	cheese
		seine	his
.20	*wohly*	wohl	well
.20	*ghast*	Gast	guest
		hast	have
.22	*starre*	starr	stiff
		starre	stare
.22	*girtel*	Gürtel	belt, girdle
.31	*faengers*	Fänger	catcher; hunting knife
.32	*obening*	oben	above, upstairs
.33	*alltogotter*	Götter	gods
.36	*hereis*	her	hither
		Reis	rice
		Eis	ice
350.1	*catz*	Katz'	cat
.2	*garerden*	gar	cooked; even
		Erden	earth
.7	*O'Dungaschiff*	Schiff	ship
.9	*gengstermen*	gestern	yesterday
		eng	narrow
.16	*elter*	Eltern	parents
		älter	older
.29	*crimsend*	Krim	Crimea
.32	*allbegeneses*	genesen	cured, become well
.34	*komnate*	komm	come
.35	*schnapsack*	Schnaps	gin
351.1	*dumm*	dumm	stupid
.6	*leibsters*	Leib	body
		Leibwache	bodyguard
		Liebster	dearest
.8	*engrish*	eng	narrow
.12	*tsingirillies'*	Grille	cricket
.13	*poppyrossies*	Roß	steed
.14	*Bissbasses*	biß-	bite
.36	*wolk*	Wolke	cloud
352.5	*brichashert*	brich	break

.6	scharlot	Schar	crowd
.7	flurtation	Flur	field, meadow
.12	meest	Mist	garbage
		mies	miserable, weak
.24	Umsturdum	stur	stubborn
		dumm	stupid
.25	sieger besieged	Sieger besiegt	victor conquered
.31	geselles	Geselle	companion, journeyman
353.3	souber	sauber	clean
.9	Senonnevero	Nonne	nun
.10	grafe	Graf	earl, count
.11	bedattle	Dattel	date (fruit)
.15	Unknun	nun	now
.17	wollpimsolff	woll-	wish
		Wolle	wool
.19	Igorladns	Laden	shop; drawer
.20	armer	Armer	poor one
.21	rockrogn	Rock	jacket, skirt
		Roggen	rye
		Kragen	collar
		Roggen	rye
.22	grosning	groß	great
.23	grunder	Gründer	founder
.29	Raum	Raum	space, room
.29	mordern Atems	Mord	murder
		modern	mould, decay
		Atem	breath
.31	Oldanelang's	lang	long
.34	birstol	Bürste	brush
354.3	stark	stark	strong
.12	Mauses'	Maus	mouse
.18	falter or mormor	Falter	butterfly
		Vater	father
		Marmor	marble
.20	fest	fest	firm
		Fest	party, holiday
.24	mutthering	Mutter	mother
		Hering	herring
.25	murdhering	Hering	herring

.25	mouldhering	Hering	herring
.28	lobed	lob-	praise
.29	traublers	Traube	grape
.31	flossim	Flossen	fins
		floß	flowed
.32	lucifug	Fug	right, reason
.33	bettle	Bett	bed
		bettel	beg
.35	fatt	Fett	fat
355.27	scuffeldfallen	Feld	field
.28	hersirrs	Herrscher	ruler, master
		irr-	mad, erring
.30	stummock	stumm	dumb, silent
.31	Khummer-Phett	Kummer	worry, sorrow
		Fett	fat
356.1	faust	Faust	fist
.2	ilkermann	Mann	man
.3	kopfinpot	Kopf	head
.5	sollecited	soll	should
.5	grobbling	grob	coarse
.8	Jura	Jura	jurisprudence
.13	wheile	weil	because
.14 f	byspills	Beispiele	examples
.15	hurtig	hurtig	nimble
.17	frishfrey	frisch	fresh
		frei	free
.18	brodhe	Brot	bread
.23	notcase	(lit.) Notfall	emergency case
.24	Packen	packen	grab, pack
.35	everwhalmed	Halm	blade, stalk
357.1	grobsmid	Grobschmied	blacksmith
.2	chowdar	schau da	look there
		dar	there
.5	forengistanters	eng	narrow
		ist	is
		Tante	aunt
.8	wear mine	Wehrmann	soldier
.11	finker	Fink	finch; rake, jolly fellow
.16	*Kunstful*	kunstvoll	ingenious, artistic

.21	turmbing	Turm	tower
.25	selvischdisch-dienence	ich dien	I serve
		dienen	serve (plural)
.30	Eonochs	noch	yet, also
358.7	giftname	Gift	poison
.22	gryffygryffygryffs	Griff	handle, hold
		-griffig	-handed
.26	woksed	wachs-	grow
.29	draken	Drachen	dragon
.35	drogueries	Drogerie	drug store
359.4	bessermettle	besser	better
7.	wassand	was	what
		Wasser	water
.10	naclenude	nagelneu	brand new
.10	cohlorine	Kohl	cabbage
		Kohle	coal, carbon
.11	bittstoff	bitte	please
		Stoff	material, matter
.14	flaus	flau	lukewarm, stagnant
.25	hofdking	Hof	court
.33 f	haydyng	Haydn	(composer)
		Ding	thing
.34	waldalure	Wald	forest
.36	gang	Gang	gait, going
360.2	floflo	Floh	flea
.7	mere Bare	Meyerbeer	(composer)
.8	beethoken	Beethoven	(composer)
.9	badchthumpered	Bach	(composer)
.9 f	gluckglucky	Gluck	(composer)
		Glück	luck
		glücklich	happy, lucky
.10	bark	Bach	(composer)
.10	bay duol	B	flat (music)
		dur	major key
.12	sweetmoztheart	Mozart	(composer)
361.2	nix	nix, nichts	nothing
.2	fears	vier	four
.16	nossowl	naß	wet

.17	ung gels	Engel	angel
.21	Onzel	Onkel	uncle
.21	grootvatter	Großvater	grandfather
362.8	tarponturboy	Tür	door
.10	soldr	Sold	wage, salary, pay
.16	garzelle	gar	cooked
		Zelle	cell
.31	hoarsehaar	Haar	hair
363.10	rasing	rasen	rage, rave; race
.14	papelboy	Pappel	poplar
.17	sprit	spritz	spray, fizz
.17	baccon	Backen	cheeks
.17	bis	biß	bit
		bis	until
.34	hintering	hinter	behind
364.6	valinnteerily	Teer	tar
.8	Shaum	Schaum	foam
.8	Baum's	Baum	tree
.18	apoclogypst	Gyps (arch.)	plaster
		gibst	give
.19	recreuter	Kräuter	herbs
		reu-	rue, regret
		Euter	udder
.20	abwaited	abwarten	wait
.28	vannflaum	wann	when
		Flaum	fluff, down
.28	merkins	merken's	notice it
.29	undher	und her	and forth
.29	Basast	Ast	branch
.33	mundamanu	Mund	mouth
.34	druck	Druck	pressure, print
365.1	herwayferer	her	this way, forth
.6	groont	Grund	ground, reason
.8	warst	warst	(you) were
.9	lieberretter	Liebe	love
		lieber	dear
		Retter	savior
.13	bauck	Bauch	belly
.14	aswarmer	Warmer	homosexual
.18	bad	Bad	bath

.21	dhamnk	dank	thank
.21	shenker	schenk	give, make a present
		Schenke	tavern, dive
.22	Hinther	hin	thither
.23	hant by hont	Hand	hand
		bei	next to
.25	Gurk	Gurke	cucumber, pickle
.28	von	von	of
.28 f	voon der pool	von der	of the
		wundervoll	wonderful
366.1	Popottes	Popo	posterior
.9	buntad	bunt	vari-colored
.13	mitsch for matsch	Mischmasch	hotchpotch
		mit	with
		misch-	mix
		Matsch	mash, mud
.17	Milcho Melekmans	Milch	milk
		melk-	to milk
		leck-	to lick
.25	feldt	Feld	field
.27	Torrenation	Tor	gate; fool
.27	upkurts	abkürz-	shorten
.31	rote	rote	red one
367.23	fare fore forn	fahre vor	drive on, pass
		vorn	ahead
.25	empores	empor	upward
		empör-	enrage, anger; revolt
.28	breide	Brei	porridge
		beide	both
.29	langwid	lang	long
368.7	tonnerwatter	Donnerwetter	thunderweather (expletive)
		Tonne	ton, barrel
		Watte	cotton wool
.8	wandly	Wand	wall
.10	arraky	Arrak	arrack (rice drink)
.20	poots	Pute	hen
		Putz(frau)	char (woman)

.20	allerthings	allerdings	indeed
.22	Zumschloss	zum Schluß	finally, at the end
		Schloß	castle; lock
.24	wisehight	Weisheit	wisdom
.32	stackle	Stachel	quill, thorn
.36	Ned?	Net? (dial.)	Isn't that so?
369.1	tuffbettle	bettel-	beg
		Bett	bed
.2	hinterhand	Hinterhand	back of the hand
.3	backturns	(lit.) zurückkehren	return, turn back
.11	Erchdeakin	Erchtag (dial.)	Tuesday
.11	Rode	rode	root out
.12	Fert Fort	fährt fort	rides away
.20	wandshift	Wand	wall
.27	Schelm	Schelm	rogue, swindler
370.4	grievingfrue	Fru (dial.)	wife, woman
		früh	early
.7	ungeborn	ungeboren	unborn
.18	Treamplasurin	Traum	dream
.20	rothole	rot	red
.21	Mollanny	moll	minor key
.28	Lochlunn	Loch	hole
.30	polisignstunter	Polizeistunde	legal closing hour
.31	bauchees	Bauch	belly
.33	smutsy floskons	schmutzig	dirty
		Floskeln	flourishes, fine writing
371.4	clucken	Glocken	bells
.6	sieguldson	sie	she
		Sieg	victory
		Siegel	seal
.17	sture	stur	stubborn
.18	bedower'd	bedauert	regrets, is sorry for
.22	Burgearse	Burg	fortress
		Bürgers	of the citizen
.24	probenopubblicoes	Proben	rehearsals
.24	clamatising	Reklame	advertising
.28	farwellens	Wellen	waves
372.1	hircomed	herkommen	arrive, come here
.2	mausers	Maus	mouse

.3	toller	Toller	mad one, wild one
.3	dotter	Dotter	egg-yolk
.4	Wanst	Wanst	belly, paunch
.6 f	engenerand	eng	narrow
		Rand	edge
.7	barttler	Bart	beard
		Bettler	beggar
.19	hemptyempty	Hemd	shirt
.23	lundsmin	Landsmann	fellow countryman
.31	Wacht	Wacht	guard
373.12	Horkus	horch	listen
.14	rassembling	Rasse	race, breed
.14	bearfellsed	Fell	skin, pelt
		Fels	rock, cliff
.22	Reinette	rein	pure, clean
		nett	nice
.22	mine	mein	my
.29	Lodenbroke	Loden	coarse woollen cloth
374.6 f	Radlumps	Radlampen	bicycle lights
.7	Lencs	links	left (direction)
		Lenz	(playwright)
.18	dorfy	Dorf	village
375.3	anker	Anker	anchor
.3	Noordeece	nur dies	only this
.12	gell	gell (dial.)	isn't it?
.16	kitz	kitzel	tickle
.19	woxen up	aufwachsen	grow up
.19	wecker	Wecker	waker; alarm clock
.26	hosy	Hose	pants
.31	fern	fern	distant
.31	So nimb	so nimm	do take it
.32	dew	du	you
.34	talor	Taler	(coin)
376.2	MacKundred	mach kund	make known
.5	wollan	Wolle	wool
		wollen	wishing
.8	voterloost	Vater	father
		Wanderlust	wanderlust

.11	dringing	dring-	throng, pierce
		dringend	urgent
.11	undergang	Untergang	sinking, ruin
.12	strenging	streng	stern; exert
.14	Sauss	Saus	rush, storm
.16	Nichtia	nicht	not
		Nichte	niece
.17	Neffin	Neffen	nephew
.33	kinn	Kinn	chin
.36	soullfriede	Friede	peace
377.10	schlymartin	Schlei	tench (fish)
		schlimm	very bad, wicked
		Schleim	mucous, slime
		Arten	kinds
.26	myterbilder	Bilder	pictures
.28	segnet	segnet	bless
.29	hin. Nup.	hinab	downward
.31	Amohn	Mohn	poppy
		ohn-	without
.33	aaskart	Aas	carrion
		Karte	map, card
378.4	gotliness	Gott	God
.6	truh	Truhe	storage chest
.8	flashmurket	Fleischmarkt	meat market
.10	. . . traum . . .	Traum	dream
.14	Magtmorken	macht	makes
		mag	like, want
		Magd	maid
		Morgen	tomorrow, morning
.14	Kovenhow	wohne	reside
		(read backwards)	
.19	Putsch	Putsch	revolutionary outbreak
.21	Geh tont	getönt	sounded, echoed, tinged
		geh	go
.24	edelweissed	Edelweiß	(flower)
		edel	noble
		weiß	white
		weißt	know

.24	idol worts	eitel Wort	vain word
.26	gurk	Gurke	pickle, cucumber
.26	frayshouters	Freischütz	free-archer, marksman; (opera by Weber)
.27	spucks	spuck	spit
.30	unbewised	unbewiesen	unproved
		unbewußt	unconscious
.36	Mahnung	Mahnung	warning
379.7	hosetanzies	Hose	pants
		Tanz	dance
.17	rheinbok	Rhein	Rhine River
		Rehbock	roebuck
		Bock	he-goat
.21	woll	woll-	want
.24	rubiny	Rubin	ruby
381.4	Hauburnea's	Haube	bonnet, hood
.21	starkened	stark	strong
		stärken	strengthen
.22	lerking	Lerche	lark
382.19	accomondation	Mond	moon
.28	Nattenlaender	Länder	countries
		-länder	(suffix indicating man of such and such a country)
383.1	*quarks*	Quark	curd; rubbish, trifle
.1	*Muster*	Muster	pattern, paragon
.5	*uns*	uns	us
.18	smacked	schmeckte	tasted
.18	kuss	Kuß	kiss
.23	Dubbeldorp	Dorf	village
384.5	ahoykling	kling-	sound
.17	Augusburgh	Auge	eye
		Burg	fortress
.26	rufthandling	ruft	calls
		Handlung	action, plot
.28	sexfutter	sechs	six
		Futter	fodder
		Futt (vulg.)	vagina
385.14	tribluts	Blut	blood

.7	wald	Wald	forest
.18	Pawerschoof	erschuf	created
.21	numbur	ur	original
387.2	Aferican	Affe	ape
.5	cheapshein	schein	appearance; shine
.11	hayastdanars	Ast	branch
		Wolken	clouds
.14	manausteriums	Ministerium	ministry
		Auster	oyster
21.	barmaisigheds	Barm	yeast
		Mais	corn
.28	Merkin	merken	notice
.31	Saman	Samen	seed
.35	Mind	mein	my
388.2	Kram	Kram	rubbish
.3	Wehpen	weh	woe
.3	luftcat	Luft	air
.4	mild aunt Liza	mild und leise	(Tristan love-death aria)
.4 f	Fulfest	fest	firmly
.5	behent	behend	nimble
.8	Fing	fing	caught; started
.14	tolls	toll	mad, extreme
.18	floot	Flut	flood
.26	silvestrious	Silvester	New Year's
.34	gerachknell	Rache	revenge
		Krach	crash, argument
		Knall	shot, report
		Geräusch	noise
389.7	Flure	Flur	meadow, floor
.13	bis	bis	until
.33	toten	Toten	the dead
390.4	Lagener	Lagen	situations,positions
391.5	Hohannes	Johannes	John
.8	hing	hing	hung
.9	borstel	Bürste	brush
		Borste	bristle
		-borst-	crack
.16	Herrinsilde	Herrin	mistress
		Insel	island

.18	giamond's	Mond	moon
.21	bronnanoleum	Bronn	spring, well
.30	Rosse	Rosse	steeds
.31	rom	Rom	Rome
392.11	doed	Tod	death
.15	Achoch	ach	oh
		Hoch	high, hail!
.16	sorgy	Sorge	sorrow, care for
.25	Kamen	kamen	came (plural)
.31	Bristolhut	Hut	hat
393.8	Bargomuster Bart	Bürgermeister	mayor
		Muster	pattern, paragon
		Bart	beard
.12	griesouper	Gries Suppe	semolina soup
.16	hosenbands	Hosenband	belt, garter
.32	oerkussens	Ohr	ear
		Küssen	kisses
.32	armsaxters	Achsel	armpit
.34	rusten	rüsten	arm, equip for war
.35	gastspiels	Gastspiel	performance by guest ensemble
394.15	Foehn	Föhn	South wind
.26 f	Engrvakon	eng	narrow
.28	kinne	Kinne	chins
395.4	analist	List	cunning, trickery
.12	oben	oben	over, upward
.23	opering	Oper	opera
.28	poot	Pute	hen
396.6	meng	menge	mix
		Menge	crowd
.12	unhomy	(lit.) unheimlich	uncanny
397.1	overflauwing	flau	lukewarm
.5	asthore	Ast	branch
.23	Amensch	Mensch	human being
.34	regul	regel	control, regulate
398.1	Mul	Müll	garbage
.2	Podex	Podex	posterior
.5	braceoelanders	Öl	oil
		anders	otherwise, differently

.15	Farfassa	Verfasser	author
.27	sehehet	sehe	look
		sehet	look (plural)
		Ehe	marriage
403.2	elf kater	elf	eleven
		Kater	tom-cat; hangover
.3	Hork	horch	listen
.12	blautoothdmand	blau	blue
.15	veilch veilchen	weich	soft
		Veilchen	violets
.16	aal	Aal	eel
404.6	hummers	Hummer	lobster
.20	shoulthern	Schultern	shoulders
405.23	maltsight	Mahlzeit	repast; conventional greeting before or after a meal
406.6	gaulusch	Gaul	horse, nag
.9	Kitzy Braten's	Kitze	goats, kids
		Braten	roast
.15	eyer	Eier	eggs
.20	rheingenever	Rhein	Rhine River
.24	nachtingale	Nacht	night
		Nachtigall	nightingale
.30	Vanhungrig	hungrig	hungry
.34	biestings be biestings	Biest	beast
407.4	smag	mag'	likes
.4	lecker biss	Leckerbissen	delicacy
.6	gross and ganz	(im) großen und ganzen	by and large, (lit.) great and whole
.9	sproke	sprach	spoke
.17	frish	frisch	fresh
.30	overgestern	(analogue to *übermorgen*, day after tomorrow)	day before yesterday
		vergeß-	forget
		Stern	star
.35	briefs	Brief	letter
.36 f	hesternmost	gestern	yesterday
		Stern	star

.15	Weh	Weh	woe, pain
.15	yeh	jäh	sudden, violent
.19	lofobsed	Obst	fruit
.28	Badeniveagh	baden	bathing
.34	coolinder	lind	soft, gentle
		linder-	soothe, tranquillize
409.17	Poumeerme	Meer	sea
.21	fortnichts	fort	away
		nichts	nothing
.29	sabotag	Tag	day
410.23	Emailia	Email	enamel
.29	moreboy	Mohr	Moor, negro
.33	eilish	eilig	hurried
411.11	pfife	Pfeife	pipe, whistle
.17	*mit*	mit	with
.26	ily	Eile	hurry
.35 f	freudful	Freude	joy
412.9	phausdheen	Haus	house
.28	safty	Saft	juice
.34	Welsfusel	Wels	(Austrian town)
		Fusel	bad brandy, gin
.35	sindybuck	Sündenbock	scapegoat
413.6	shuft	Schuft	scoundrel
		schuft-	work hard
.13	pilgarlick	pilgerlich	like a pilgrim
.20	sophykussens	Küssen	kisses
.22	mund	Mund	mouth
.34	rubiny	Rubin	ruby
.34	winklering	Winkel	angle, corner
		wink-	wink, beckon, wave
414.2	Anders	anders	otherwise
.19	husstenhassten . . .	Husten	cough
		Haß	hate
		hast'n	have a
.22	akkant	Kant	(philosopher)
		Kante	edge
.25	Floh	Floh	flea
.25	Bienie	Biene	bee
.25	pupa-pupa	Puppe	doll
.26	langtennas	lang	long

.28	ameng	Menge	lot of, crowd
415.6	o'shouker	Zucker	sugar
.7	whaal	Wal	whale
		Wahl	choice, selection
.10	beck	Becken	pelvis, bowl
		Beck (dial.)	baker
.12	langsome . . .		
	langsome	langsam	slow
.13	mutter	Mutter	mother
.13	duffmatt	matt	lifeless, mate
			(chess)
.16	uns	uns	us
.20	Fudder	Vater	father
		Futter	fodder
.21	ally looty	alle Leute	everyone
.25	bagateller	Teller	plate
.26	zeit	Zeit	time
.27	sommerfool	Sommer	summer
		Sommervogel	butterfly
.29	Nixnixundnix	nix (nichts)	nothing
		und	and
.33	Nefersenless	Fersen	heels
.35	tile	teil	divide, part
		Anteil	share
416.3	weltall	Weltall	universe
.3	raumybult	Raum	space
.4	bynear saw . . . wee	beinah so . . . wie	almost as . . . as
.4	schelling	Schelling	(philosopher)
		Schelle	bell; handcuff
.4	kopfers	Kopf	head
.4 f	sair sair	sehr	very
.5	making spaces	Spaß machen	make jokes,
			have fun
.6	laus	Laus	louse
.10	wetting	wetten	bet
.11	durrydunglecks	Unglück	misfortune,
			accident
		leck-	lick, leak
.11	horing	hören	listen
.12	*ichnehmon*	ich nehm' an	I assume

.12	*diagelegenaitoikon*	die Gelegenheit	the opportunity; affair
.13	sieck	siech	infirm
.14	for grub	vergrab-	bury
		grub	dug
.15	wist gnit	wis nit (weiß nicht)	does not know
.16	dry	drei	three
.16	spint	spinnt	is mad, raving
.16	volomundo	Mund	mouth
.17	Nichtsnichts- undnichts	nichts und	nothing and
.21	lustres	Lüster	chandeliers
.23	mundballs	Mund	mouth
.25	neutriment	neu	new
.29	grillies	Grille	cricket; whim, sad thought
.33	hegelstomes	Hagel	hail
		Hegel	(philosopher)
.35	tegolhuts	Tegel	bluish green marl
		Hut	hat
.35	ruching	(Ge)ruch	smell
		rutschen	slide
417.1	spuk	spuck	spit
		spuk	haunt; uproar
.1	Graussssss! Opr	Graus	horror
		Oper	opera
.4	smetterling	Schmetterling	butterfly
.9	umsummables	umsumm-	buzz around
.11	Gross	groß	great
.13	farfalling	verfallen	disintegrate
.17	Floh	Floh	flea
.18	Bieni	Biene	bee
.22	schneezed	Schnee	snow
.23	eyeforsight	Eifersucht	jealousy
.24	aspinne	Spinne	spider
.25	spass	Spaß	fun, joke
.26	spizzing	spitzig	acute, sarcastic
		spritzen	squirt
.28	ameising	Ameisen	ants
		Meise	titmouse

.29	Floh	Floh	flea
.30	Bienie	Biene	bee
.30	jucking	jucken	itch
.30	jukely	jucke-	itch
418.1	Weeps	Wespe	wasp
.8	impfang	Empfang	reception, welcome
		empfang	received, welcomed
		impfen	vaccinate
.8	mine wideheight	meine Weisheit	my wisdom
.14	*Floh*	Floh	flea
.14	*Bienie*	Biene	bee
.20	*horsegift*	Gift	poison
.28	*beseeked*	besiegt	conquered
		besucht	visited
419.4	*Sulch*	solch	such
.4	*soveal*	so viel	so much
		sowohl	as well as
.12	velktingeling	welk-	withered
		geling-	succeed
.14	wandervogl	Wandervogel	bird of passage (youth movement)
420.9	kookin	Kuchen	cake
.27	Roofloss	ruf-	call, shout
		floß	flowed
.33	Milchbroke	Milch	milk
		Brücke	bridge
.33 f	Traumcondraws	Traum	dream
.35	Shown geshotten	schon geschossen	already shot
421.7	Understrumped	Strumpf	stocking
.10	ab, Sender	Absender	sender, shipper
.27	irelitz	Irrlicht	will o' the wisp
		Eier	eggs
		Litz-	braid, lace
422.3	fleischcurers	Fleisch	meat
.3	Gach	gack-	cackle
		ach	oh
.7	brach	brach	broke
.29	Baden	baden	bathing
.32	liliens	Lilien	lilies
.32	veldt	Welt	world

.34	Wucherer	Wucherer	usurer
423.10	Hock	hock-	squat
.16	prhose	Hose	pants
.18	Grundtsagar	Grund	ground; reason
		sag-	say
		sogar	even
.19	eggschicker	schick-	send
.33	negertop, negertoe,	Neger	Negro
	negertoby		
.33 f	negrunter	Neger	Negro
		runter	downward, down
.36	Bro Cahlls	bröckle	crumble
424.1	Bruda	Bruder	brother
.1	Brat	brat-	roast
.9	Prost bitten	Prost!	To your health!
		bitten	ask for, plead
.12	cram	Kram	rubbish
.21	. . . bau . . .	bau-	build
.22	. . . krinmgern . . .	Krim	Crimea
		gern	gladly
.28	sucker	Zucker	sugar
.28	Mildbut likesome	mild und leise	(Tristan love-death aria)
.33	silbils	Silbe	syllable
425.9 f	muttermelk	Muttermilch	mother's milk
		melk-	to milk
		Melk	(Austrian town)
.15	allergrossest	allergrößte	largest of all
.18	pinsel	Pinsel	painter's brush
.22	soamheis	heiß	be called, hot
.31	papst	Papst	pope
426.7	krenfy	Kren	horseradish
.17	Ally bully	alle balle (dial.)	all gone
.21	wieds	wie	how
.27	dreamskhwindel	Windel	diaper
		Kindel	little child
427.1	linkman	links	left (direction)
.6	spoorlessly	spurlos	without a trace
.7	popo	Popo	posterior
.12	luftstream	Luft	air

.14	sharmeng	Schar	crowd
		Menge	crowd
.18	it is to bedowern	es ist zu bedauern	it is regrettable
.19	mine bruder	mein Bruder	my brother
.21	undfamiliar	und	and
.23	toll	toll	wild
.24	soo ooft	so oft	so frequent
.32	Spickspooks-spokesman	spick	smoke (meat)
		spuck-	spit
		spuk-	haunt
428.21	shiff	Schiff	ship
429.5	hosen	Hosen	pants
.13	altered	älter-	to age
430.20	sie	sie	she
.20	bie	Biene	bee
431.33	gesweest	Geschwister	siblings
432.9	offrand	Rand	edge
.16	buckling	bucklig	humpbacked
		Bückling	kipper
		bück-	bow, stoop
.26	feugtig	Feuchtigkeit	moisture, damp
.32	bekant	bekannt	known, famous
433.20	bisbuiting	biß	bite
.26	sassers	saß	sat
.31	ern	er	he
434.13	forestand	Vorstand	chairman
		Verstand	reason, understanding
.14	tillgive	(lit.) zugeben	admit
.24	hose	Hose	pants
435.14	jaeger	Jäger	hunter
.15	Suzy's Moedl's	süße Mädels	sweet girls
.23	hemel	Himmel	heaven
.28 f	milchmand	Milchmann	milkman
436.9	kosenkissing	kosen	caress
.12	. . . magd	Magd	maid
.24	2bis	bis	until
437.1	gastricks	Strick	rope
.30	kommen	kommen	coming

.30	olt	alt	old
.31	maul	Maul	muzzle
438.26	unleckylike	lecke	lick
439.7	friar's	Freier	suitor
.13	tante's	Tante	aunt
.23	sludgehummer's	Hummer	lobster
.33	hijiniks	Genick	neck
.36	*Standerd*	Erd-	earth
440.5	nazional	Nazi	national socialist
.12	Linzen	Linsen	lentils; lenses
		Linz	(Austrian city)
.25	hemd	Hemd	shirt
441.6	Poposht	Popo	posterior
		Poscht (Swiss)	post-office
.13	Die	die	the
.15	taucht	taucht	dipped, submerge
.28	buel	Bühl	hill
		Bühel	humpback
442.1	fremdling	Fremdling	stranger
.6	enoch	noch	more, yet
.18	markt	Markt	market
.28	sicker	sicher	sure, secure
.32	blizz	Blitz	lightning
.36	louseboob	Lausbub	rascal
443.4	bubby	Bubi	lad
.12	magistrafes	strafe	punish
.14	federal	Feder	feather
.21	flurewaltzer	Flur	meadow, floor
		Walzer	waltz
.25	stortch	Storch	stork
.29	Rhoss's	Roß	steed
.30	pubpal	Pöbel	rabble
444.11	Forstowelsy	Forst	forest
.15	vokseburst	wachse	grow
		bürst-	brush
.26	minners	Minne	love
.31	Annybettyelsas	Bett	bed
.32	ging	ging	went
.32	Ganger	Gänger	walker
.35	doll	toll	mad, extreme

.35	homeseek	(lit.) heimsuchen	afflict, punish
445.6	ask unbrodhel	Aschenbrödel	Cinderella
.13	rebmemer	Rebe	vine
.13	mottob	tob-	rage, play violently
		Motte	moth
		ob	whether
.31	doppeldoorknockers	doppel	double
.32	Ostelinda	Ost	East
		Linde	lime tree
.34 f	Toobliqueme	bequem	comfortable
446.9	mitch	mich	me
.11	zuccherikissings	Zucker	sugar
.18	touf! touf!	tauf-	baptize
447.9	Haarington	Haar	hair
.21	wateringplatz	Platz	place, square
		platz-	burst, split
448.22	Loos	Los	fate, fortune
.31	Badanuweir	Baden	bathing
449.16	frind	Rind	beef
.21	maurdering	Mauer	wall
.23	brilliants	Brilliant	diamond
.28	hoerrisings	hör-	hear
		reisen	travel
450.17	juckjucking	juck-	itch
.31	heimlocked	Heim	home
		lockt	beckons, allures
.34	wage	wage	dare
451.4	cold strafe illglands	Gott strafe England	God punish England
.7	erbole	er	he
		erb-	inherit
		Bowle	spiced wine
.16	mine shatz	mein Schatz	my treasure
.16	funk	Funk-	spark
.24	brut	brut-	brood, hatch
452.1	luftsucks	Luftzug	draft
		Luftsack	air-pocket
.2	borting	Borte	edge, border
.7	earnst	ernst	earnest

.7	Schue	Schuh	shoe
453.6	hering	Hering	herring
.16	Sommers	Sommer	summer
.22	Po	Po	posterior
.34	Deck	deck-	cover
.34	diamants	Diamant	diamond
454.2	welt	Welt	world
.3	trost	Trost	consolation
.3	alms	Alm	mountain pasture
.4	Haugh! Haugh!	Hoch!	hurrah!
		hauch-	breathe
.9	blossy	bloß	bare
.22	sternish	Stern	star
.23	what's loose	was ist los?	what is going on?
.29	gang	Gang	gait, walk
.35	pobbel	Pöbel	rabble
455.10	di'yegut	gut	good
.10	di'yesmellygut	gut	good
.11	di'yesmelly-patterygut	gut	good
.11	Joe Hanny's	Johanna	Jean, Joan
.22	neuthing	neu	new
.24	daum	Daumen	thumb
.26	Afterpiece	After	hindquarters
.29	Notshall	Not	need, emergency
		Schall	resonance, sound
456.10	lout	laut	loud, sound
.16	bloomancowls	Blumenkohl	cauliflower
.22	clingleclangle	Klingel	bell, ring
		klingklang	ding-dong
457.9	grame	Gram	grief, affliction
.15	drawhure	Hure	prostitute
.28	flusther	flüster	whisper
.36	witwee's	Witwe	widow
458.1	witween	Witwe	widow
.16	obote	Bote	messenger
		Boote	boats
		U-Boote	submarines
.35	praxis	Praxis	practice

459.3 f	msch! msch!	mische	mix
		Mensch	man
.20,21	betrue	betreue	care for, nurse
.21	betreu	betreue	care for
		treu	loyal
.27	atem	Atem	breath
.27	Obealbe	ob	whether
460.11	simself	Sims	cornice
.16	ulmost	Ulm	elm
.20	Jungfraud's	Jungfrau	virgin
.20	Messongebook	Meßbuch	missal
.25	hearz'waves	Herz	heart
.26	von	von	of
461.14	heimlick	heimlich	secretly
.23	isonbound	Eisen	iron
		Eisenbahn	railway train
.26	whesen	Wesen	being
462.10	snowybrusted	Brust	breast
.17	Dancekerl	Kerl	man, guy
.26	froubadour	Frau	woman
.29	Ousterrike	Österreich	Austria
		Auster	oyster
.30	swits	Schwitz-	Swiss, sweat
463.6	Magnaffica	Affe	ape
.24	Rossya	Roß	steed
.33	Famose	famos	splendid
.34 f	prisonpotstill	Postille	book of family sermons
464.6	flamme	Flamme	flame
.7	*Shervos*	Servus	(greeting)
.10	Thunderweather	Donnerwetter	thunderstorm (expletive)
.10	khyber schinker	kaibe, cheibe	(Swiss expletive)
		Schinken	ham
.20	pfeife	Pfeife	pipe, whistle
.21	yunker	Junker	young aristocrat
.22	wanked	wanken	stagger
.22	awriting	reiten	ride
.27	Auster	Auster	oyster
.28	Hungrig	hungrig	hungry

.30	Freeshots	Freischütz	free-archer; (opera)
.30	Feilbogen	feil	venal, mercenary
		Pfeil	arrow
		Bogen	bow
.31	Grab	Grab	grave
.34	breastlaw	Breslau	(city)
.36	You rejoice me	(lit.) du erfreust	you make me glad
		mich	
465.7 f	Weih...		
	shamewaugh	Weih	kite, hen-harrier
		Weihrauch	incense
.8	wip	Weib	wife, woman
.10	biss	bis	until
		biß	bite
.25	leberally	Leber	liver
.30	racist	ist	is
.30	rossy	Roß	steed
466.18	jubalharp	Jubel	jubilation
.22 f	foreboden	verboten	forbidden
		Boden	floor; attic
.28	Bitrial	(lit.) Zweikampf	duel
.29	holmgang	Holmgang	duel to the death
.29 f	Fee gate has Heenan	Wie geht es Ihnen	How are you
	hoity, mind uncle	heute, mein	today, my dark
	Hare?	dunkler Herr?	sir?
.35	stones	stöhnen	groan
467.6	bissing	biß	bite
.12	onkel	Onkel	uncle
.14	yuonkle's	Onkel	uncle
468.8	Toughtough	tauf-	baptize
.9	shingeller	Geller	one who yells,
			calls shrilly
.17	blink	blick	look
.30	hoodies	Hode	testicle
.36	hourihaared	Haar	hair
469.7	staffet	Stafette	relay race
.12	nettly	nett	nice
.14	mutther	Mutter	mother
.16	Groenmund's	Mund	mouth
.20	danked	dank-	thank

.21	Linduff	lind	gentle, soft
.23	nimmer	nimmer	never
.23	siskinder	süße Kinder	sweet children
.27	Adry	drei	three
470.13	jourd'weh	Weh	woe, pain
.13 f	Guesturn's lothlied	gestern	yesterday
		Lied	song
.15	esaltarshoming	Esel	donkey
.18	phantastichal	tast-	touch
		Stich	stitch, prick
.25	weiners	Weiner	one who cries
		Wein	wine
.36	widdershins	Wiedersehen	see again
		Widder	ram
		Widersinn	contradiction
.36	Frida	Frida	dim. of Friederike
		Friede	peace
471.6 f	widerembrace	wider-	mutual, again
.16	stadion	Stadion	stadium
.19	fahr	fahr	ride, drive
.21	wind hound	Windhund	grayhound; thoughtless boy
.31	hellyg	Helligkeit	clarity, lightness
.35	Haun	Hahn	cock
473.3	Sylvester	Sylvester	New Year's
475.2	foorchtha	Furcht	fear
.23	klettered	klettert	climbs
.24	spoor	Spur	trail, trace
.34	kuss	Kuß	kiss
.35	kuss cley	Kuß	kiss
		Klee	clover
476.6	Asnoch	noch	yet
.13	fallen	Fallen	traps
		Fall	case
477.5	alannah	nah	near
.30	melding	melden	announce, register
.33	Ecko	Ecke	corner
478.8	Esellus	Esel	donkey
.10	wald	Wald	forest
.10	wand	Wand	wall

.11	teerm	Teer	tar
.12	tartallaght	lacht	laughs
.13	torpentine	Tor	gate, fool
.14	grossgrown	groß	big
.16	plankgang	Gang	passage, walk
.21	*clee*	Klee	clover
.30	sohohold	hold	handsome
.31	houn	Huhn	chicken
.34	fogloot	Glut	embers
.35	duck	Tag	day
479.17	bloss	bloß	bare
.21	austers	Auster	oyster
.29	Weissduwasland	weißt du was? (echoes Goethe's „Kennst du das Land")	you know what?
.32	Draken	Drachen	dragon
.33	Hennu	Henne	hen
		nu	now
.33	ab laut	Ablaut	vowel-gradation
		laut	loud
.34	Beseek	besuche	visit
.35 f	ganghorn	Gang	walk, gait
.36	Warum night	warum nicht	why not
480.4 f	Folchu! Folchu!	folge	follow
		falsche	the wrong (false) one
.16	Futtfishy	Futter	fodder
		Futt (vulg.)	vagina
.17	enkel	Enkel	grandson
.20	Easterheld	Held	hero
.23	wrynecky fix	Reinecke Fuchs	Reynard the Fox
		neck-	tease
.28	Dyb! Dyb!	Dieb!	Thief!
.36	Wolfgang	(middle name of Goethe, who wrote „Reinecke Fuchs")	
481.5	*Dies Eirae*	Dies' Ei	this egg
.9	Sinflowed	Sintflut	sin flood

.9	Befurcht	befürcht-	fear
.10	tristich	Stich	stitch, stab
.14	from yours	(lit.) von deinem	of yours
.15	lavast	Ast	branch
.17	ob	ob	whether
.18	brauchbarred	brauchbar	useful
		Brauch	custom
		brauch-	need, use
		Bart	beard
.20	Hellig Babbau	hell	light
		heilig	holy
		Bau	build, building
.21	Ei	Ei	egg
.28	Noctuber	über	over
.33	brodar	Bruder	brother
.34	pfander	Pfänder	distrainer, bailiff
.34	pfunder	Pfund	pound
.34	furst	Fürst	prince
482.3	Hau's	hau-	beat, hit
.7	Haltstille	Haltestelle	bus- or tram-stop
		halt	stop
		Stille	silence
.14	donkeyschott	danke schön	thank you
.16	Hooshin	huschen	slip away, scatter
.16	hin	hin	thither
.17	stepschuler	Schüler	pupil
483.1	altereffects	Alter	age, old man
.3	Shaum	Schaum	foam
.15	Fierappel	vier	four
.15	Nwo, nwo!	wo	where
.19 f	unwachsibles	wachs	grow
.22	kalblionized	Kalb	calf
.24 f	altermobile	Alter	age
.25	Been ike	bin ich	was I, am I
.25	hins	ins	in the
		hin	thither
.25 f	kindergardien	Kinder	children
		dien	serve
.27	meis enfins	Mais	corn
		Meisen	titmice

.28	fromming	fromm	pious
		frommen	avail, benefit
.29	plage	Plage	plague, vexation
.30	eltered	Eltern	parents
484.8 f	then ersed	dann erst	only then
.9	irredent	irre	confused, crazy
.9 f	beggelaut	Laut	sound, tone
		laut	loud
.15	none meer	nunmehr	henceforth
.25	langways	lang	long
.29	leabhour	Lieber	dear one
		Liebhaber	lover, fancier
485.1	Sagart	Sag-art	manner of saying
.1	nilobstant	Nil	Nile River
		Lob	praise
		ob	whether
		Obst	fruit
.3	Itch dean	ich dien	I serve
.3	Sauer	sauer	sour
.7	alleman: Suck at!	alle Mann	everyone
		suchet	search
.10	Ichthyan	ich dien	I serve
.13	sprakin sea	sprechen Sie	Do you speak
	Djoytsch?	Deutsch?	German?
.13	Bleseyblasey	blas-	blow
		Blase	blister
		blaß	pale
.24 f	Wanstable	Wanst	belly
.26	nightmale	Nachtmahl	supper
.27	your innereer'd	erinner	remember, remind
.27	heerdly	Heer	army
		Erd-	earth
.28	heer	Heer	army
.33	shepulla-		
	mealahmalong	lahm	lame
486.1	Halt	halt	hold, stop
.6	owldfrow	Frau	woman, wife
.6	lied	Lied	song
.8 f	understudium	Studium	studies, curriculum
.14	armer	Armer	poor one

.21	horizont	Horizont	horizon
.26	sey	sey (modern: sei)	be
.27	trenned	(ge)trennt	separated
.28	sternly	Stern	star
.34	irmages	irr-	confused, mad
487.17	gots	Gott	god
.29	gangin	(ge)gangen	went
.30	Gangang	Gang	walk, gait
488.15	aver	aber	but
.20	ostralian	Ost	East
.26	nein	nein	no
.26	Punk	Punkt	period
489.2	fuchs	Fuchs	fox
.9	Tass	Tasse	cup
490.3	wehicul	Weh	woe
.8	Gottgab	Gott	god
		gab	gave
		Gabe	gift
.14	gabgut	gab	gave
		gut	well
.17	doblinganger	Doppelgänger	double
		Döblin	(writer)
.18	erstwort	erst	first
		Wort	word
.20	Stauter	stau-	stow away, dam up
.27	redtettetterday	rette	rescue
491.2	sag	sag	say
.4	silbings	Silben	syllables
.12	mittle	Mittel-	middle
.14	turturs	Tür	door
.14	raabraabs	Rabe	raven
.18	*Mansianhase*	Hase	rabbit
.19	*aff*	Affe	ape
.21	Braudribnob's	Brau	brew
		Braut	bride
.21	bummel	Bummel	stroll, promenade
.28	blutchy	Blut	blood
.35	Bygrad	Grad	degree
492.1	voice	weiß	know
.3	womit	womit	with which

.7	faulscrescendied	faul	lazy, rotten
.9	rusish	Russisch	Russian
.10	Wolossay's	Waller See	(lake)
.14 f	saxy luters	Sechseläuten	Zurich spring festival
		Leute	people
.18	pilsens	Pilsen	(city)
.22	Hairductor	Herr Doktor	doctor
.24	wasserguss	Wasserguß	downpour, sink
		Erguß	effusion, overflow
.29	dry	drei	three
.29 f	dryfilthyheat	Dreifaltigkeit	trinity
.30	pinslers	Pinsler	dauber
.33	priesters	Priester	priest
493.15	bort	Bort	shelf, board
		Abort	privy
.16	whem	wem	whom
.18	fintasies	Finte	feint; fib
.19	weewahrwificle	wie wahr	how true
		wieviel	how much, how many
.20	Torquells	torkel-	totter, reel
		Tor	gate; fool
		Quelle	spring, source
.20	woolsark	Sarg	coffin
.21	heuteyleutey	heute	today
		Leute	people
.22	fiertey	vierte	fourth
.23	massstab	Maßstab	ruler, measure
.27	Eivin	Ei	egg
.35	dearast	der Ast	the branch
		die Rast	the respite, rest
494.10	Satarn's	tarn-	camouflage
.12	Merkery	merk-	notice
.14	Noth	Not	need, emergency
.17	Waddlewurst	Wurst	sausage
.19	obesendean	ob	whether
		Besen	broom
		absenden	send off
		dien	serve

.20	Emfang	Empfang	reception
.20	Shotshrift	Schrift	writing
.25	chitschats	Schatz	treasure, sweetheart
.29	kitssle	kitzel	tickle
.35	habasund	habe	have
		Hund	dog
		Sund	sound, strait
495.9	trout	traut	dear, beloved
.9	henkerchoff	Henker	hangman
.10	froren	(ge)froren	frozen
.11	Withworkers	(lit.) Mitarbeiter	colleagues
.15	slepp	schlepp-	drag
.18	Auborne	Aue	meadow
.23	maschine	Maschine	machine
.25	Elsebett	Bett	bed
.34	Frui	Frau	Mrs.
496.11	meid on	meiden	avoid
.11	hold	hold	handsome
.20	da. Da's	da	there
.24	traumaturgid	Traum	dream
.26	merchamtur	Amt	office
		Tür	door
.29	bier	Bier	beer
.29	seemly	ziemlich	rather
497.4	irrara	irre	confused, mistaken
.6	scalpjaggers	Jäger	hunter
.12 f	besogar	sogar	even
.20	bettlers	Bettler	beggar
.28	Piowtor	Autor	author
		Tor	gate; fool
.31	reiseines	Reis	rice
		Reise	trip, voyage
		seine	his
		eines	one thing
.35 f	tintanambulating	Tinte	ink
498.4	Isteroprotos	ist	is
		er	he
.7	halle	Halle	hall
		halle	resound
.7	fhroneroom	Fröner	serf, vassal

.12	Athclee	Klee	clover
.14	epheud	Efeu	ivy
.14	granddaucher	Taucher	diver
		auch	also
.18	oels	Öl	oil
.23	clayroses	Klee	clover
.23	Ogonoch	genug	enough
		noch	yet, more
.26 f	ringcampf	Ringkampf	wrestling match
.33	chilidrin	drin	inside
499.7	Boese	böse	evil
.7	Mord	Mord	murder
.7 f	Smirtsch	Schmerz	pain
.8	Smertz	Schmerz	pain
.8	Woh	wo	where
		Weh	woe
.9	Thaunaton	Ton	tone, clay
.9	Eulumu	Eule	owl
.11	Mamor	Marmor	marble
.12	Psich	sich	himself
		Sicht	sight
.15	Muster	Muster	pattern, paragon
.21	tolkshap	tolkier-	paint boldly
.23	altknoll	alt	old
.33	Gar	gar	cooked; even
.33	Donnerbruck	Donner	thunder
		Brücke	bridge
		Bruch	break
500.11	Lancs	links	left (direction)
.13	linklink	links	left
		Klinke	doorhandle
.17	slagt	schlägt	beats, conquers
.21	ersther	Erster	first one
.24	Fort! Fort!	fort!	away!
501.36	mistandew	Mißstand	nuisance
		Mist	garbage
		du	you
502.1	farranoch	fahre noch	drive on, still driving
.6	westnass	naß	wet

.6	ostscent	Ost	East
.8	sprungen	(ge)sprungen	sprung
		Sprung	coition (animals)
.11	Nmr	Nummer	number
		nimmer	never
.12	highlucky nackt	(lit.) hochglücklich	very happy
		heilige Nacht	holy night (Christmas)
		nackt	naked
.14	geallachers	Gelächter	laughter
.18	hice	heiß	hot
.18	calid	kalt	cold
.20	hellstohns	hell	bright, sharp
		stöhn-	groan
.20	flammballs	Flamme	flame
.33	phunkel	funkel	spark
.33	mares	mehr	more
503.8	kikkinmidden	Kücken	chick
.10	Ealdermann	der Mann	the man
.10	Junkermenn	Junker	young aristocrat
		Männer	men
.13	bidetree	beide	both
.14	Astagob	Ast	branch
		Tag	day
		ob	whether
.17	tolkar	tolkier-	paint boldly
.21	Woful	wo	where
.28	sigeth	sagt	says
		sieget	conquer
.28	Warneung	warne	warn
		Warnung	warning
		neu	new
.30	eshtree	Esche	ash tree
.32	Slivenamond	Mond	moon
.33	beerchen	Beerchen	little berry
		-chen	(diminutive suffix)
504.19	Tonans	tönen	sound
.23	flamingans	Gans	goose
.35	muchmore	(lit.) vielmehr	moreover, rather
505.3	mid	mit	with

.7	whimmering	wimmer	whimper
.8	seeleib	See	sea
		Seele	soul
		Leib	body
.16	Amengst	Menge	crowd, many
		Angst	anxiety
.22	neming	nehm-	take
.23	Tod, tod	Tod	death
.29	Upfellbowm	Apfelbaum	apple tree
.32	frausch	Frau	woman
		Frosch	frog
		Rausch	intoxication
.33	fussforus	Fuß	foot
.34	knacked	knackt	cracks
.35	knechtschaft	Knechtschaft	servitude
506.5	Muster	Muster	pattern, paragon
.11	Hehr	hehr	sublime, majestic
		Herr	Mr.
.13	Wo wo	wo	where
.13	grauws	grauen	grow grey, become dawn; have an aversion to or horror of
.15	foerst	Forst	forest
		vorerst	first of all
.17	Yesche	Esche	ash tree
.24	mehrer	mehr	more
507.22	ur sprogue	Ur-Sprache	original language
.24	billet	Billett	ticket
508.17	blaff!	Blaff!	bang!
.18	leidend	leidend	suffering
.22	minnestirring	Minne	love
.33	spilling	spielen	playing, pretending
.33	knickt?	nicht?	right?
		knickt	cracks, bends
.34	Gels	gel?	right?
		Gelse	mosquito
.34	bach	Bach	brook
.34	Etoudies	tu' dies	do this

509.4	brief	Brief	letter
.11	Schaum	Schaum	foam
.20	Gaul	Gaul	horse, nag
510.9	frohim	froh	merry
.13	Shotland	Schottland	Scotland
.24	ehren	Ehren	honors
		Ähren	ears of corn
.25	Insul	Insel	island
.26	breadcost	Kost	food, diet
.35	Fraufrau	Frau	woman, Mrs.
511.1	widdershins	(auf) Wiedersehen	good-by
		Widder	ram, Aries
.8	kuckkuck	kuck	look
		Kuckuck	cuckoo
.10	bufeteer	Tier	animal
		Teer	tar
.13	leckle	lächel	smile
		leck-	lick; leak
.13	lach	lach-	laugh
.27	shubladey's	Schublade	drawer
		Schub	push
.30	klees	Klee	clover
.30	schalter	Schalter	switch; ticket window
		Schulter	shoulder
.30	sehdass	seh' daß	see that
		so daß	so that
512.2 f	Drysalter	drei	three
		Alter	age
.5	brustall	Brust	breast
.9	glancefull	glanzvoll	glittering
.11	Tollertone	toller	mad, wild
.14	safter	Saft	juice
.15	stricker	Strick	rope, noose
		Stricker	knitter
.17	cramwell	Kram	junk
.18	herreraism	Herr	gentleman, Mr.
.35	Tiltass	Tasse	cup
513.7	bulweh	Weh	woe, pain
.8	Fluteful	Flut	flood

.8	orkan	Orkan	hurricane
		Organ	voice
.11	kniejinksky	Knie	knee
.14	schraying	schrei	cry, shout
.17	Ortovito	Ort	place
.27	darm	Darm	intestine
.31	metandmorefussed	Fuß	foot
514.7	clay	Klee	clover
.8	schappsteckers	Stecker	plug
.9	Schottenly	Schott	partition wall
		Schotten	Scotchmen
		Schotter	rubble
.10	wasistas	was ist das	what is that (term used in France for peephole)
.11	Heavystost's	stößt's	it bumps
.14	nonne	Nonne	nun
.19	shuler's	Schüler	pupil
.22	Thundersday	(lit.) Donnerstag	Thursday
.27	Schott	Schotte	Scotchman
		Schott	partition, bulwark
515.3	cram	Kram	junk
.3	spick	spick-	smoke (meat)
.3	spat	spät	late
516.3	Meesta	mies	miserable
.9	loisy	Läuse	fleas
.11	naas	naß	wet
.12	nagles	Nägel	nails
.12	fex	fex-	harvest
.12 f	so fort	sofort	immediately
		fort	away
.18	wann ... wann	wann	when
.19	Fanden	fanden	found
.23	Patsch	Patsch	slap, pop, smash
.35	finister	finster	dark
517.4	dumm	dumm	stupid
.23	Pansh	pansch-	adulterate, meddle
.24	Are you of my meaning?	(lit.) Bist du meiner Meinung?	Do you agree with me?
.26	querqcut	quer	across, diagonal

.33	Amties	Amt	office
518.12	meatierities	Tier	animal
.18	ersatz lottheringcan	Ersatz	substitute
		Elsaß-Lothringen	Alsace Lorraine
		Hering	herring
518.19 f	berebelling	Beere	berry
		bellen	to bark
		Rebe	vine, grape
.19 f	berebelling	pellen	to peel
.30	Da	da	there
.31	Ab	ab	from, exit
.32	neat wehr?	nicht wahr?	right?
		wehr-	defend, fight
.35	clang	Klang	sound
519.1	cling	kling-	sound
.1	engels	Engel	angels
.1	neuropeans	neu	new
.3	pootsch	Putsch	revolutionary outbreak
.16	Finging and	fingen an	started
		fing	caught
.22	tors	Tor	gate; fool
520.6	earwanker	wank-	stagger
.9	tumple	Tümpel	puddle
.14	shielings	schiel-	squint
.14	tocher	Tochter	daughter
.15	albs	Alb	elf
.18	soldats	Soldat	soldier
.20	flutes	Flut	flood
.22	you have right	(lit.) du hast Recht	you are right
.27	Quatsch	Quatsch	nonsense
521.17 f	wizzend	Witz	wit
		witzelnd	joking
.23	freckened	frech	impudent
.32 f	What do you have?	(lit.) Was hast du?	What's wrong?
.35	moll	moll	minor key
.35	seilling	Seil	rope
522.19	nass-	naß	wet
.30	catheis	heiß	hot; be called
523.4	genewality	Wahl	election, choice

.5	pwopwo	wo	where
		Popo	posterior
.19	sagobean	sag	say
		ob	whether
		ihn	him
524.6	naturpark	Naturpark	natural preserve
.26	gut	gut	good
.26	Wissixy	wiss-	know
.30	zwelf	zwölf	twelve
525.2	Watsch	Watsche	slap, smack
.5	Tolloll	toll	mad
.8	absexed	ab-	off (prefix often implies disinclination from, or exhaustion from repeating action signified by the verb)
.17	monach	nach	after
		Monat	month
.20	es hit neat zoo?	ist es nicht so?	isn't that so?
.21	*fogeyboren Herrin*	wohlgeborene Herrin	well-born mistress
.22	*Plundehowse*	Pluderhose	wide trousers
		Landhaus	country house
.24	*freck*	frech	impudent
526.2	polster	Polster	pillow
		polster	upholster
.25	rawkneepudsfrowse	Putzfrau	charwoman
.30 f	bachspilled	Bach	brook
		Beispiel	example
		spiel	play
.32 f	weidowwehls	Weide	pasture; willow
		Wehl	bay (water)
		Weh	woe, sorrow
.33	Shieling's	schiel-	squint
		Schelling	(philosopher)
.34	shielsome	schiel-	squint
527.1	Gotellus	Gott	god
.20	knicks	Knicks	curtsy

.24	idoll	doll (toll)	nonsensical, extravagant
.25	Bortolo	Borte	edge, fringe
.27	Netta	nett	nice
.28	My rillies	Marille	apricot
		Rille	rill, groove
.28	liebeneaus	lieben	dear, to love
		Aue	meadow
.30	reinebelle	reine	pure, clean
		Nebel	fog, mist
		belle	bark (dog)
528.5	bloss	bloß	only, bare
.6	Audiens	ich dien	I serve
.6	diamants	Diamant	diamond
.6	blickfeast	Blick	look, glance
		fest	steadily
.7	minne	Minne	love
.7	hos	Hose	pants
.8	Mindelsinn	Mündel	ward, pupil
		Sinn	sense
		Mendelssohn	(composer)
.12	Magda	Magd	maid
.13	Tolka	tolkier-	paint boldly, daub
.15	thing in such	(lit.) Ding an sich	the thing in itself (Kant)
.22	e'er scheining	Schein	appearance, seeming
		Erscheinung	phenomenon (Kant)
.29	Connacht	Nacht	night
.34	nimmer	nimmer	never
529.12	assistents	Assistent	assistant
.17	Hocksett's	hock-	squat
		Hochzeit	wedding
.23	Glassthure	Türe	door
		Hure	prostitute
.24	ziel	Ziel	goal
.30	pfuffpfaffing	Pfaffe	priest, cleric
.31	scabsteethshilt	Schild	shield, sign
.34	hengster's	Hengst	stallion

.14	hoose	Hose	pants
.15	lagenloves	lagen	lay
.17	gendarm	Gendarm	gendarme
		Darm	intestine
.19	wordybook	Wörterbuch	dictionary
.19	trunchein	Hein	(personification of death)
		ein	in
.20	Roof Seckesign	ruf	call
		sechs	six
		ein	one
.20	van der Deckel	von der	of the
		Deckel	cover, lid
.31	Wallpurgies	Walpurgis	witches' meeting
.34	rost	Rost	rust; roast
531.1	disdag	Tag	day
.4	Nummer	Nummer	number
.6	kisschen	Kisschen	little pillow
		-chen	(diminutive)
.7	gansyfett	Gänsefett	goose fat
.10	Abarm's	erbarm-	take pity
.13	reinethst	reine	pure
.14	libbers	Leber	liver
.14	goulewed	Gaul	horse, nag
.15	lautterick's	laut	loud
		lauter	pure, undefiled
.16	souprette	rette	rescue
.17	jigotty	Gott	god
.25	pfortner	Pförtner	porter, turnkey; pylorus
		Pfote	paw
532.3	sinder's	Sünder	sinner
.6	Amtsadam	Amt	office, bureau
.6	heil!	heil!	hail!
.9	MacAuscullpth	aus	out
.10	Allenglisches	Englisches	English
.11	Angleslachsen	Lachs	salmon
		lachen	laugh
		Achsen	axes, axles
.11	Sall and Will	soll und will	should and will

.19	crim crig	Krim-Krieg	Crimean War
.22	Slutsgartern	Schloßgarten	palace garden
		Lustgarten	pleasure garden
.31	Floss	floß	flowed
		Floß	raft
533.4	sowell	(lit.) sowohl	so much
.15	numborines	eins	one
.15	why drive fear	zwei	two
		drei	three
		vier	four
.18	cagehaused	Haus	house
		gehaust	resided
.18	duckyheim	Heim	home
.21	Johannes	Johannes	John
.23	Kerk	Kerker	dungeon
.26	youngend	Jugend	youth
.28	parruchially	(Ge)ruch	smell
.29	Engels	Engel	angel
.32	reicherout	reicher	richer
.33	Hiemlancollin	Himmel	sky, heaven
534.8	ernst	ernst	earnest
.9	tandsel	Tand	toy, bauble
		tänzel-	skip, caper
.10	babad	Bad	bath
.18	Keisserse Lean	Kaiserling	would-be emperor
.26	Happen seen sore eynes belived?	Haben Sie so eines erlebt?	Have you experienced one like that?
.30	teppling	tepp (dial.)	senile
.30	ixits	ix	(the letter x)
.35	Steck	steck	put, stick
.35 f	Instaunton	staun	is amazed
		Ton	tone
535.2	von Hunarig	von	of
		Huhn	chicken
		Hahnrei	cuckold
.3	chry	Schrei	cry
.3	urs	ur-	original, primitive
.8	hrossbucked	Ross	steed
.9	Pferdinamd	Pferd	horse

.16	meisies	Ameise	ant
		Meise	titmouse
.17	ratshause	Rathaus	city hall
.19	Noksagt	sagt	says
.29	O. W.	Oh Weh!	oh dear!
.31	askt	Ast	branch
536.2	fernspreak	Fernsprecher	telephone
.12	Guestermed	gestern	yesterday
.13	achershous	ach	oh
.14	hoyt	heute	today
.14 f	stock of eisen	Stock	stick
		Eisen	iron
.16	bock	Bock	goat
.19	neberls	neben	next to
		Nebel	fog, mist
.20	stein	Stein	stone
.21	zober	Zuber, Zober	tub
		Ober	waiter
.22	flautish	flau	feeble, flat
		Flaute	calm, dull weather
.34	Haar	Haar	hair
.35	Mine kinder	meine Kinder	my children
.35 f	mine wohl	mein Wohl	my health, well-being
537.10	*Ehren*	Ehren	honors
.11	outbreighten	Brei	porridge
		ausbreiten	expand
.12	eng	eng	narrow
.25	illsell	Ilsel	(dim. of) Ilse (Elizabeth)
.28	verbanned	verbannt	banished
.34	Weck	weck-	wake
.36	unpurdonable	pur	pure
538.8	melkkaart	melk-	milk
.10	wert	Wert	worth
.11	naktlives	nackt	naked
.12	roohms	Ruhm	fame
.14	cansill	Kanzel	pulpit
.18	My herrings!	Meine Herren!	Gentlemen!

.20 f	saumone	Sau	sow (pig)
		Saum	seam, edge
		Samen	seed
.24	guardient	dient	serves
.24	gretched	Gretchen	Margaret
.26	Ous	aus	out
.27	freiung pfann	Freiung	wooing
		frei	free
		Pfanne	skillet
.27	rassembled	Rasse	race, breed
.28	mein	mein	mine
.29	Each habe goheerd	ich habe gehört	I have heard
.29	uptaking	(lit.) annehmend	assuming
.31	Odor	oder	or
.31	smutsick	schmutzig	dirty
.31	rivulverblott	Blatt	leaf
		Revolverblatt	scandal sheet
.32 f	Schottenhof	Schottenhof	Scotch court
		Schott	bulwark
.33	Igen	eigen	own; peculiar
539.6	A. G.	Aktien-	joint stock
		Gesellschaft	company
.11 f	cramkrieged	Kram	junk
		Krim-Krieg	Crimean War
.13	stolemines	Stollen	tunnel (mining)
.14	Spainien	Spanien	Spain
.18	Irrlanding	Irland	Ireland
		irr	confused, wrong
.19	bottlenim	nimm	take
.20	platzed mine residenze	platzt	bursts
		meine Residenz	my residence, mansion
		Residenz-Platz	capitol square
.21	burgage	Burg	fortress
.22	fimmel	Fimmel	sledge-hammer; craze
.27	siegewin	sie	she
		siege	win, conquer
		gewinne	win

.28	slauchterday	auch	also
		Lauch	leek
.28	cleantarriffs	Riff	ridge, sandbank
.29	marken	marken	to set a boundary
		Marken	postage stamps
.30	Allbrecht	brecht	break
		recht-	right
		Alberich	(guardian of Nibelung hoard)
.31	kingsinnturns	Sinn	sense, wit
		sinnt	thinks, ponders
.35	skat	Skat	(German card game)
.36	Englisch	Englisch	English
540.11	*Be suke and sie so ersed*	Besuchen Sie zuerst	first visit
		Besuche und sieh zuerst	visit and first see
.19	ist	ist	is
.20	hansbailis	Hans	Jack
.22	meet	mit	with
.24	gaingangers	Gänger	walker
.28	Been so free	bin so frei	permit me, I take the liberty
.29	Thank you, besters!	Danke bestens!	Many thanks!
.29	Hattentats	hatten	had
		Tat	deed
		Attentat	assassination attempt
.29	mindered	minder	lessen
.29	Blaublaze	blau	blue
		Laub	foliage
.33	midday's mallsight	Mittagsmahlzeit	midday meal
		Mahlzeit!	good appetite!
.34	ludd in	lud ein	invited
.34	waldy	Wald	forest
.35	luft	Luft	air
.36	segn	segn-	bless

541.1	habt	habt	have
		(ge)habt	had
.4	Thursitt	Ursitte	primitive custom
		Sitte	custom
.4	chort	Ort	place
.5	Michan	mich	me
.6	tors	Tor	gate; fool
.8	grossscruple	groß	big
		Rüpel	lout
.13	Sirrherr	Herr	sir
.14	Paybads	Bad	bath
.15	matt	matt	defeated, exhausted
.15	papst	Papst	pope
.15 f	onfell	Anfall	attack, seizure; inheritance
		(lit.) auffall-	are noticeable, remarkable
.17	Berueme to	berühmt	famous
.21	wegschicked	wegschick-	send away
.21	Wellinghof	Hof	court
.25	fastbroke	fast	almost
.25	Neederthorpe	nieder	lower
.26	slobodens	Boden	floor, attic
.27	bathandbaddend	badend	bathing
.31 f	murmel	Murmel-	murmur, whisper
.33	fluted	Flut	flood
.35	ofen	Ofen	oven
.35 f	meckling of my burgh	Mecklenburg	(part of Germany)
		meckern	bleat
542.1	reized	reiz-	irritate, charm
.1	murphyplantz	Pflanze	plant
		Platz	place, square
.5	rainelag	lag	lay
.8	Putzemdown	putz	clean, scrub, adorn
.8	Kommeandine	komme	come
.12	obtemperate	ob	whether
.13	meckamockame	meck-	bleat
.21	schwalby	Schwalbe	swallow (bird)
		Schwall	flood (of words)

.34	jingelbrett	gelb	yellow
		Brett	board
		rett-	rescue
543.9	feshest	fesch	elegant, smart
.10 f	palastered	Palast	palace
		Laster	vice
.11	vonderbilt	von der	of the
		Bild	picture
.16	Ostmanorum	Ost	East
544.1	Zetland	zet	the letter z
545.13	herrors	Herr	gentleman
.23	snuffbuchs	Buch	book
		Büchse	box
.27	morgenattics	Morgen	morning; tomorrow
.29	debelledem	belle	bark (dog)
		dem	to the
.30	domstered	Dom	cathedral
.34	graben	Grab	grave
		Graben	trench; to dig
546.1	obstain	ob	whether
		Obst	fruit
.4	flister	flüster	whisper
		List	cunning
.5	frish	frisch	fresh
.17	dubildin	du	you
		Bild	picture
.22	reclam	Reklame	advertising
.29	Taubiestimm	taubstumm	deaf & dumb
		Taube	dove
		Biest	beast
		Stimme	voice
.31	wiening	Wien	Vienna
547.11	Tollollall	toll	mad, extravagant
		lall-	stammer, babble
.17	lacksleap	Lachs	salmon
.19	rivierside	vier	four
.20	Flott	flott	fast, buoyant
		Flotte	fleet of ships
23.	upreized	(lit.) aufreißen	tear up
		reiz-	irritate, charm

.24	stock	Stock	stick
.25	rookwards	rückwärts	backwards
.26	domfine	Dom	cathedral
		Dampf	steam
.27	baresark	Sarg	coffin
.29	bryllupswibe	Brille	eye-glasses
		Weib	wife
.29	hallthundered	hall-	resound
.30	arsched	Arsch	ass
.32	streng	streng	stern
.33	ringstresse	Ringstraße	circular boulevard
.35	imorgans	immer	ever
		im Organ	in the voice
		Morgen	tomorrow
		Gans	goose
.35	ervigheds	er	he
		Ewigkeit	eternity
.36 f	dampfbulls	Dampf	steam
548.1	Lettland	Lettland	Latvia
.4	uns	uns	us
.4	shyblumes	Blume	flower
.7	whiles I herr	weil	because
		sei	be
		Herr	master
.7	amstell and been	umstellen	alter, change about
		Amtsstelle	public office
		anstelle	instead of
		bin	am
.8	chambrett	Brett	board
.9	hochsized	Hochzeit	wedding
		hoch	high
		Ochs	ox
.10	when	wenn	if
.12	ankerrides	Anker	anchor
.12	freipforter	frei	free
		Pforte	gate, door
.12	huts	Hut	hat
.13	foregather	(lit.) versammel-	assemble
.14	sumbad	Bad	bath

.14	farseeker itch my list	versichere ich	I insure, assure
		versuche ich meine List	I try my cunning
.15	dogshunds'	Hund	dog (Dachshund)
.17	umgyrdle	umgürtle	girdle
.20	lilienyounger	Lilien	lilies
		Jünger	disciple
.22	stockinger's	stocken	stammer
.33	swanchen's	Schwänchen	little swan
549.1	Cunnig's	König	king
.1	Soll leve! Soll leve!	Soll leben!	hail!
.22 f	stabmarooned	Stab	staff
.24	sankt	Sankt	Saint
550.1	bissed	biß-	bite
.9 f	knobby lauch	Knoblauch	garlic
.11	gothakrauts	Kraut	cabbage, herb
.15	dampkookin	Dampfküche	steam-kitchen
.18	powlver	Pulver	powder
.32 f	Pruny-Quetch	quetsch-	squeeze
		Zwetsche	plum
551.1	windtor palast	Tor	gate, fool
		Winterpalast	winter palace
.2	elenders	elend	miserable
.2	lubded	(Ge)lübde	vow
		lobtet	praised
.3	chauffed	kauft	buys
.3	fuesies	Füße	feet
.3	Wigan's	Wiegen	cradles
.5	thronsaale	Thronsaal	throne-room
.5	lecking	lecken	lick
.7	merk	merk-	notice
.8	littleritt	ritt	rode
.9	tinsel and glitter	Hänsel und Gretel	(fairy tale)
.11	foredreamed	verträumt	lost in reverie
.11 f	fullmaked	Vollmacht	full power, power of attorney
.15	prater	Prater	(Viennese park)
.24	minne	Minne	love
.25	astrolobe	lobe	praise

.25 f	erdcloset	Erd-Klosett	earth privy
.28	festfix	fest	firmly
		(lit.) feststellen	determine, establish
.29	gottalike	Götter	gods
		göttlich	divine
.36	Voter, voter, . . . voter	Vater	father
552.2	Debwickweck	weck	wake
		Weg	way, away
.5	stonefest	fest	solid
.7	Astralia	Ast	branch
.11	Cassels	Kassel	(city)
.12	Vnost	Ost	East
.16	Welhell	Walhalla	(home of gods)
.19	Neeblow's	Nebel	fog
		Nibelung	(Siegfried's followers)
.20	eltering	Eltern	parents
.21	ewigs	ewig	ever, eternal
.25	oragel	Orgel	organ
.29	sass her nach	saß	sat
		hernach	afterwards
.31 ff	Hoke!	Hoch!	Hail!
.35	snaeffell	Fell	hide, fur
553.3	alderbirk	Birke	birch-tree
.3	tannenyou	Tannen	pines
.11	turisses	Tür	door
		Risse	gaps, tears
.14	eiligh	eilig	hurried, quick
.22	hallaw vall	Walhalla	(home of gods)
.27	lindub	lind	soft, gentle
.27	froh	froh	merry
.30	nordsoud	Nord	North
.34	fahrts	Fahrt	journey
.34	velkommen	willkommen	welcome
		von	of
		Wagen	car
.35	Hoseyeh	Hose	pants

.35	Roamer Reich's	Römerreich	Roman Empire
554.1	turnintaxis	Thurn und Taxis	(family)
.10	Mattahah	matt	exhausted
.10	Joahanahanahana	Johann	John
		Johanna	Jean, Joan
		nah	near
555.1	whaas	was	what
.5	naket	nackt	naked
.7	kinderwardens	Kinder	children
.10	titranicht	nicht	not
		Nacht	night
.21	bald	bald	soon
.24	rhubarbarorum	Rhabarber	rhubarb
556.20	stilled	still-	silence, soothe; wean
.23	nacht	Nacht	night
.23	Wachtman	wacht	wakes, guards
.24	punkt	Punkt	period, exactly
.25	curserbog	Kursbuch	train schedule
.25	grassgross	groß	big
.25	bumpinstrass	Straße	street
.25	henders	Hände	hands
.26	pubbel	Pöbel	rabble
.29	gnasty	Gnas-Fest	Austrian carnival party, masquerade
.29	brillers	Brille	eye-glasses
.29	knappers	knapp	tight
		Knappe	apprentice, candidate for knighthood
.30	strumpers	Strumpf	stocking
.30	sminkysticks	Schminke	make-up
.30	eddiketsflaskers	Etikett	bottle-label
		Flasche	bottle
.32	Kothereen	Kot	dirt, filth
.35	schritt be schratt	Schritt	step
		Schrat	hobgoblin, imp
557.2	Welks	welk	wilted

.6	hapspurus	Habsburg	(Austrian ruling family
		Spur	trail
.10	fingerhals	Hals	neck
.10	clookey	Klo (Klosett)	privy, water closet
.10, 11	tocher	Tochter	daughter
558.28	beautifell	Fell	fur, pelt
.30	hodypoker	Hode	testicle
559.6	clubsessel	Sessel	chair
.21 f	Say! Eh? Ha!	(apes German pronunciation of Earwicker's initials)	
		C, E, H	(C, E, B in German musical notation)
.22	Matt	matt	exhausted
.24	homoplatts	platt	flat, low, vulgar
		Platz	place
560.5	Spill	spiel	play
.14	ingang	Eingang	entrance
.15	Lingling, lingling	(German onomatopoetic description of bell ringing or water falling)	
.16	ephort	Ort	place
.18	begraved	begraben	buried
.20	bloombiered	Bier	beer
.21	fordone	(lit.) vertan	wasted, scattered
.24	on this wise	(lit.) auf dieser Weise	in this way
.25	hayamatt peruke	Heimat	home
		matt	exhausted
		Perücke	wig
.29	papel	Pappel	poplar
.34	togive	(lit.) zugeben	admit
.34	tonearts	Tonart	musical key
561.2	knifekanter	Kante	edge
.6	Ah so?	Ach so?	Really?
.16	brooder's	Bruder	brother
.17	friendeen	Freunde	friends
		Freundin	girlfriend, mistress

.19	flocaflake	Flocke	flake
562.3	es ma	ist mein (dial.: es min)	is my
.3 f	barytinette	nette	nice
.4	gift	Gift	poison
.7	Allaliefest	Allerliebst	dearest
		lief	ran
.15	Platsch	platsch	splash
.17	twobis	bis	until
.25	buchel	Buch	book
563.15 f	tintingface	Tintenfaß	inkpot
.23	blizky	Blitz	lightning
.29	barmhearts	barmherzig	charitable, compassionate
.31	rosengorge	Rosen	roses
.31	greenafang	fang-	catch
		Anfang	beginning
.31	Blech	Blech	tin
564.16	man	man	one
.20	tallworts	Wort	word
.22	tannoboom	Tannenbaum	pine-tree
.24	weald	Wald	forest
.34	bodom	Boden	bottom, floor
		Dom	cathedral
.35	gardeenen	Gardinen	curtains
565.2	Holl Hollow	hall-	resound
.2	guttergloomering	Götterdämmerung	twilight of the gods
.6	Whervolk	Volk	people
.6	dorst	Durst	thirst
.10 f	guineeser	genese	regain health
		Genießer	sensualist
.11	beutel	Beutel	bag
		Beute	booty
.11	staub	Staub	dust
.11	To feel, you?	Zu viel, ja?	Too much?
.13	brainskin	(lit.) Gehirnhaut	meninges
.22	grossman's	groß	big
.27	*nikte*	nickte	nodded
.31	seling	Seele	soul

.34	to visit	(lit.) zu Besuch	as a guest
566.22	wappon	Wappen	insignia
.29	Hummels	Hummel	bagpipe; romp
		Himmel!	heavens!
.32 f	finister	finster	dark
.35	verst	erst	first
567.5	With a such	(lit.) mit einem	with such an . . .
		solch . . .	
.9	grosses	großes	a big thing
.18	knechts	Knecht	servant, groom
.25	faxes	Faxen	buffoonery
.26	poblesse	Pöbel	rabble
.27	overall	überall	everywhere
.30	souftwister	sauft	guzzles
.32	durst	Durst	thirst
.34 f	Tollacre, tollacre	toll	mad, wild
.36	guelflinks	flink	quick
		links	left (direction)
568.1	Mauser	Maus	mouse
.9	sonneplace	Sonne	sun
.11	sweet from her	(lit.) süß von ihr	sweet of her
.12	a meise	Ameise	ant
		Meise	titmouse
.13	ist	ist	is
.13	tear on	Tyrann	tyrant
.17	boorgomaister	Bürgermeister	mayor
		Mais	corn
.21	meng	Menge	crowd
		meng-	mix
.23	Dom	Dom	cathedral
.28	cabbuchin	Buch	book
.28	Caubeenhauben	Hauben	hoods
569.1	tonguespitz	Spitze	tip
		spitz	sharp
.2	balkonladies	Balkon	balcony
.4	gluckspeels	Glücksspiel	game of chance
		Glückspilz	lucky fellow
.8	Aposteln	Aposteln	apostles
.14	umclaused	um-	(prefix:) around
		Klaus-	hermitage, cell

.17	Dock, dock	doch, doch	oh yes
.21	mealsight!	Mahlzeit	Good appetite!
570.5	dollmanovers	doll	wild
		Manöver	maneuver
.12	Morganas war	morgen	tomorrow
		war	was
.14	soundpicture	(lit.) Tonbild	tone poem
.14 f	It gives furiously	Es gibt . . . zu	that makes one
	to think	denken	think
.18	say him	(lit.) sag ihm	tell him
.27 f	Forthink	(lit.) verdenk	blame
571.1	brilling	Brille	eye-glasses
.1	say me	(lit.) sag mir	tell me
.3	blend	blend-	dazzle
		blendend	splendidly
.7	can	kenn-	know
.7	lese	lese	read
.14	ivytod	Tod	death
.36	toadcavites	Tod	death
572.2	hinterclutch	hinter	behind, back-
		Hinterhalt	ambush
.3	heartpocking	pochen	beat, knock
.4	youngfries	Jungfer	maiden
.4	backfrisking	Backfisch	teen-age girl
.5	spick and spat	spick-	smoke (meat)
		spät	late
573.28	Viteilius	teil	part, divide
.33	lax	Lachs	salmon
574.4	Brerfuchs	Fuchs	fox
.15	Wieldhelm	Wilhelm	William
575.32	prepoposal	Popo	posterior
.34	treuson	treu	loyal
576.18	boomooster	Muster	paradigm
		Baumeister	master-builder
.20	straxstraightcuts	stracks	directly
.34	roamers	Römer	Romans
.36	magdalenian	Magd	maid
577.1	Morionmale	-male	-times; scars, traces
.4	bissemate	Bisse	bites
.10	biber	Biber	beaver

.11	hose	Hose	pants
.13	fahrman	fahr-	travel, drive
		Fährmann	ferryman
.14	elf	elf	eleven
.17	hodinstag	Hoden	testicles
		ins	in the
		Tag	day
.17	fryggabet	Freigabe	release, setting free
		Gebet	prayer
.18	feme	Feme	secret court
.29	sengentide	sengen	singe, singing
.29 f	unterlinnen	unter	under
		Linnen (Leinen)	linen
		Unter den Linden	(Berlin street)
.33	strangfort	Strang	hangman's rope
		fort	away
.34	dryflooring	(lit.) Trockenboden	drying-loft
578.3	Oom Godd his villen	um Gottes Willen	for God's sake
		Villen	villas
.6	pharrer	Pfarrer	priest
.11	O'Sorgmann	sorg-	sorrow, worry
		Mann	man
.13	fuchser	Fuchs	fox
.13	schouws	schau	look
.19 f	Donauwatter	Donau	Danube
		Donnerwetter	thunderweather (expl.)
		Watte	cotton wool
.22 f	Happy tea area, naughtygay frew!	Habe die Ehre, gnädige Frau!	(conventional salutation, roughly: I have the honor, gracious lady!)
.28	brennt	brennt	burns
.34	aller	aller	of all
.36	konyglik	königlich	royal
579.8	boot	bot	offered
		Boot	boat
.14 f	raabers	Rabe	raven
.20	freund	Freund	friend

580.2	zollgebordened	Zollgebühr	import duty
		geboren	born
.4	werfed	werf-	throw
		Werft	shipyard
.13	qual	Qual	torture
.13	himmertality	Himmel	heaven
		immer	always, eternal
.17	seegn	segn-	bless
		siegen	conquer
.36	leud	Leu	lion
581.2 f	vehmen's	Vehme, Feme	feud
.22	awlus	alles	everything
.32	alter	Alter	age; old man
.33	anander	einander	another, each other
.34	emmerhim	immerhin	in spite of everything
583.11	twillingsons	Zwilling	twin
.20	Irryland	irre	confused, crazy
		Irland	Ireland
584.21	kikkery key	kikiriki	cockadoodledoo
.25	morgans	morgens	in the morning
.27	Cocorico	kikiriki	cockadoodledoo
.32	tochters	Tochter	daughter
.34	chorecho	Chor	chorus
585.3 f	choree choroh choree chorico	Chor	chorus
		roh	rude, raw
.8	brief	Brief	letter
.8	dankyshin	dankeschön	thank you very much
.11	paratonnerwetter	Donnerwetter	thunderweather (expl.)
.12 f	pity shown	bitteschön	you're welcome
.18	inyeborn	eingeboren	innate, inborn
.22	Humperfeldt	Feld	field
.24	donahbella	nah	near
.24	Totumvir	tot	dead
.27	abjourned	ab-	off, from
586.7	Omama	Omama	grandmother
.13	ding	Ding	thing

.20	anywas	irgendwas	anything
.22	sammel	sammel	gather
.23	riviers	vier	four
.24	gangs	Gang	walk, way
.25	roamer's numbers	Römer	Roman
	ell a fee		
		elfe (dial.)	eleven
.27	mean fawthery	(Swiss:) Min Vater	my father is from
	eastend appull-	ischt en Appe-	Appenzell
	celery	zeller	
.28	Seekersenn	Senn	cowherd
		sicher sein	be secure
.29	hoonger	Hunger (apes Gm.	hunger
		pronunciation)	
.29 f	mac siccar	mach' sicher	make sure
.30	goodsforetombed	Gottverdammte	accursed
	ereshiningem	Erscheinungen	apparitions
.31	thuncle's	dunkel	dark
.34	wand	Wand	wall
587.2	Loab at cod then	Lobet Gott den	praise God the Lord
	herrin	Herrn	
		Herrin	mistress
10.	wouldower	Waldhauer	wood-cutter
.16	blucher	Blücher	(Prussian marshal)
.26	daintylines	-lein	(diminutive suffix)
.29	foregathered	(lit.) versammelt	gather together
.33	burgomaster	Bürgermeister	mayor
588.5	wappin stillstand	Waffenstillstand	armistice
		Wappen	insignia
.8	frush	Frosch	frog
.16	hofd	Hof	court
		hofft	hopes
.17	welkim	welchem	to which
		welken	wilt
.20	wolken	Wolken	clouds
.28	Esch so eschess	Esche	ash-tree
.33	humbild	Bild	picture
.34	erewold	Urwald	jungle
589.7	milliards	Milliarde	billion
.20	Ofter	öfter	often

590.1	sinflute	Sintflut	sin-flood
.10	reignbolt's	Regenbogen	rainbow
.15	formast	Ast	branch
.19	yetst	jetzt	now
.19	hin	hin	thither
.20	for true	(lit.) fürwahr	indeed
.29	Tag	Tag	day
.30	Tiers, tiers and tiers	Tier	animal
593.3	wohld	wohl	well
.6	Tass, Patt	Tasse	cup
		Patt	stalemate
.8	Sonne feine	Sonne	sun
		feine	fine
.9	Guld	Gulden	(coin)
.13	The leader,	Lieder	songs
	the leader		
.17	pewtewr	P. T. Publikum	audience, clientele
	publikumst		(P. T. is conventional abbrev. on placards for *praemissis titulis*)
.23	Nuseht	nu	now
		seht	sees
594.2	Dah	da	there
.2 f	umprincipiant	um-	about, around
.5	astamite	Ast	branch
.7	kal	kahl	bald
.13	See but!	(lit.) Sieh' nur!	Have a look!
.14	Respassers	Spaß	fun, joke
.14	Meins	mein	my
.15	Peins	Pein	pain, torture
.16	mengle	meng-	mix
.16	flasch	Flasche	bottle
.17	rasch	rasch	quickly
.17	pasch	Pasch	dice
.18	tanderest	Tand	toy, trifle
.18	rosinost	Ost	East
.21	totouches	tot	dead
.25	frohn	froh	merry
		fron-	holy

.25	Overwhere	über(all)	everywhere
.30	han	Hahn	cock
.30	Sassqueehenna	Henne	hen
595.1	Ostbys ... ost	Ost	East
.3	knock and knock	nach und nach	by and by
.3	nachasach	nach	after
		Sache	affair
.4	langscape	lang	long
.4	strauches	Strauch	bush
.7 f	goodbett	Bett	bed
.8	wassing	was	what
.10	Newirgland's	würg-	strangle
		wir	we
		Irland	Ireland
.10	korps	Körper	body
		Korps	corps
.16	armaurs	Mauer	wall, battlement
.16	waglugs	wag-	dare
		lüg-	lie, falsify
.17	homdsmeethes	Hemd	shirt
.23	hoseshoes	Hose	pants
596.1 f	milchgoat	Milch	milk
.5	ersekind	Kind	child
.13	oel	Öl	oil
.14	angalach	lach-	laugh
.15	fert in fort	fährt ihn fort	drives him away
.32	pfan	Pfanne	skillet
.36	Goute	gut	good
597.5	hundrund	Hund	dog
		rund	round
.11	ist	ist	is
.13	Djinpalast	Palast	palace
.20	lucksloop	Lachs	salmon
.25	Vayuns	uns	us
.26	risy fever	Reisefieber	nervousness before a journey
.29	weltr	Welt	world
		Wetter	weather, storm
.29	wirbl	Wirbel	whirl, agitation
598.3	Forswundled	verschwunden	disappeared

.6	Nil	Nil	Nile
.7	allburt	-burt	birth
.10	ghastern	gestern	yesterday
.10	morgning	morgen	tomorrow
.33	Grossguy	groß	big
599.1	orts	Ort	place
.4	Vartman	wart-	wait
.4	pfath	Pfad	path
.5	pfunded	Pfund	pound
.5	vatars	Vater	father
.5	Himmal	Himmel	heaven
.8	fattafottafutt	Futter	fodder
		Futt (vulg.)	vagina, buttocks
.20	tache	Tasche	pocket, bag
.22	tarn	Tarn	mask, camouflage
600.5	saft	Saft	juice
.12	Viggynette	nette	nice
.13	Neeinsee	nee (nein)	no
		nie	never
		ein	in, a
		See	sea
.15	Fane	Fahne	flag
.26	immermemorial	immer	always
.29	*Elochlannensis*	Loch	hole
.30	Pfif	Pfiff	whistle
.34	feist	feist	corpulent
.34	ferial	Ferial-	holiday
.35	celibrate	brate	roast
.36	beatend	-end	(participial suffix)
.36	hutcaged	Hut	hat
601.1	bisnisgels	bis	until
.2	offrand	Rand	edge, hem
.3	Pfaf	Pfaffe	priest
.6	wasseres	Wasser	water
.8	Hwo	wo	where
.8	Asthoreths	Ast	branch
.10	Hillsengals	seng-	singe
		Engel	angel
.13	clanagirls	kleine	little

.20	clangalied	Klang	sound, tone
		Klagelied	lamentation
		Lied	song
.26	Ringsingsund's	rings	around
		Sund	sound (water)
.27	Waidafrira's	Waid	blue dye
		friere	freeze
.28	unloud	unlaut-	impure
		Umlaut	vowel modification
.30	naeme	nehme	take
.31	meidinogues	meiden	avoid
602.4	flowerfleckled	werf-	throw
		Fleck	spot
		leck-	lick
.13	hall	hall-	sound, echo
.24	Schulds	Schuld	guilt
.30	steerner	Sterne	stars
.31	Hurr	Herr	Mr.
603.4	Schoen! Shoan!	schön	good, pretty
		schon-	already; spare, protect
.4 f	Shoon the Puzt!	Schuhe geputzt	shoes polished
.9	Eilder	eil-	hurry
.10	dass is it duss	daß	that
.10	singen	singen	singing
.10	sengers	senge-	singe
		Sänger	singers
.11	trow	trau-	trust, dare
.14	alter	älter	older
.16	Hans	Hans	Jack
.19	plushfeverfraus	Frau	woman
.22	fleece in	fließen	flow
.24	foos	Fuß	foot
.32	hunt	Hund	dog
604.4	Heremonheber	Heber	lifter, lever
		Anheber	instigator
.8	theirinn	Irin	Irish woman
		rinn	flow, gush
.8	Besoakers	Besucher	visitors
.8	loiter	Leute	people

.14 f	fartykket plan	fahr-	travel, ride
		Fahrkarte	ticket
		Fahrplan	schedule, itinerary
.16	elderens	Eltern	parents
.25	insels	Insel	island
.26	Osthern	Ost	East
		Ostern	Easter
605.29	ubidience	dien	serve
606.13	Bisships	Biß	bite
.15	blixom	blickst	look
.18	cobbold	Kobold	goblin
.27	kuvertly	Kuvert	envelope
.27	falted	falte-	fold
.31	wandler	wandl-	transform, cast a spell
.31	rute	Rute	wand, switch
.32	utterrock sukes	Unterrock	petticoat
		such-	search
.36	geen we gates	gehen	go
		wie geht's?	how are you?
.36	tofatufa	tauf-	baptize
607.4	sonner	Sonne	sun
.8	behing	behing	covered, decorated
.14	segnall	segne	bless
.18	Gnug	genug	enough
.22	engl	Engel	angel
.24	schlimninging	schlimm	bad, evil
.24	summerwint	Wind (d pron. t)	wind
.25	regn	Regen	rain
.25	durknass	durchnäss-	soak, wet through
.28	Frist	Frist	time limit
.28		frißt	devours, eats
.30 f	Boergemester	Bürgermeister	mayor
.31	Eisold	Eis	ice
608.16	motther	Mutter	mother
		Motte	moth
.20 f	beckerbrose	Bäcker	baker
		Brösel	crumbs
.24 f	ohahnthenth	Hahn	cock
		ahnt	suspects

.29	*Sorte*	Sorte	kind, sort
.29	hundled	Hund	dog
609.10	Weisingchetaoli	weis-	wise; show, direct
.10	levellaut	laut	loud; sound
.11	Rosina	Rosine	raisin
.18	Hillewille	Wille	will, desire
.18	Wallhall	Walhalla	(home of gods)
.19	Obning	ob	whether
.28	Dies	dies	this
.28 f	tonobrass	Ton	tone
.31	wolk	Wolke	cloud
610.5	Fing Fing	fing	caught
.12	holf	-holf-	helped
.14	velleid	Wehleid	self-pity
		Leid	suffering, sorrow
		Eid	oath
.20	Wartar wartar	warte	wait
.20	Wett	wett-	bet
.22	Winne	(ge)winne	win
611.9	fast	fast	almost
.18	heupanepi	Heu	hay
.21	Ding hvad in idself id est	Ding an sich	thing in itself
.24	obs	ob	whether
		Obst	fruit
.24	epiwo	wo	where
.28	hemhaltshealing	Helmholtz	(scientist)
.32	throughsighty	(lit.) durchsichtig	transparent
.33	Uberking	über	over, super
.35	holmgrewnworsteds	Holm	hill
612.3	Exuber	über	over, super
.4	Ober	ober	over
		Ober	waiter
.11	kirikirikiring	kikiriki	cockadoodledoo
.13	hueglut	Glut	embers, glow
.15	sennacassia	Senn	cowherd
.15	Sukkot	Kot	filth
.16	Punc	Punkt	period
.16	whackling	wacklig	tottering

.23	sager	Sager	sayer
		Säger	sawyer
.23	eruberuption	erober-	conquer
		über	over
.31	bygotter	Götter	gods
613.2	Halled	hallt	resounds
.9	Feist	feist	corpulent
.10	our scheining	Erscheinung	appearance, phenomenon
.11	farbiger	farbig	colored
.25	amess in amullium	Ameisen	ants
		Müll	garbage
.28	folgor	Folger	follower
.30 f	ortchert	Ort	place
614.6	rolle	Rolle	roll; role
.8	mournenslaund	Morgenland	the Orient
		Laune	mood
.9	forders	förder-	advance, implement
		forder-	demand, challenge
615.4	mutter	Mutter	mother
.16	uhrweckers	Uhr	clock
		Wecker	alarm clock
.25	beamstark	stark	strong
.32	Stringstly	strengstens	strictly
616.4	widming	Widmung	dedication
.9	threi	drei	three
.12	Monacheena	China (Gm. pron.)	China
.25	Wolkmans	Wolke	cloud
617.2	hose	Hose	pants
.16	brand	Brand	fire
.16	Fing! One	fing an	started
		fing	caught
.17	aging	ging	went
.18	gutmurdherers	gut	good
.21	will commen	willkommen	welcome
.31	fands	fand	found
618.2 f	handsel for gertles	Hänsel und Gretel	(fairy tale)
619.4	grocerest	größer	bigger
		größest-	biggest
.5	parzel	Parzelle	parcel (land)

.12	holth	Holz	wood
.17	fetted	fett	fat
.29	goolden	Gulden	(coin)
620.4	buckly	Buckel	hump
.4	Rosensharonals	Rosen	roses
.16	sehm asnuh	seh-	see
		nu	now
.16	bredder	Brüder	brothers
.23	widdle	Windel	diaper
621.4	fing	fing	caught
.6 f	rucksunck	Rucksack	rucksack
.14	roost brood	Rostbrot	toast
622.7	po	Po	posterior
.25	Wald	Wald	forest
623.3 f	mutthergoosip	Mutter	mother
.16	vom	vom	of the
.17	Hungerig	hungrig	hungry
.22	Clatchka	klatsch-	applaud; gossip
.36	traumscrapt	Traum	dream
624.2	mugisstosst	stoßt	bump
.5	dunner	Donner	thunder
.20	lewdy	Leute	people
625.15	fern	fern	far
.15	rasstling	Rasse	race, breed
		Rast	rest
.19	Mch	mich	me
.20	Dom	Dom	cathedral
.27	dumblynass	naß	wet
.27	sama sitta	Samen	seed
		Sitte	custom
626.10	fad	fad	boring
.31	uspart	spart	saves
.32	espart	erspart	saves up
627.3	Imlamaya	im	in the
628.9	toy fair	Täufer	baptist
.12	behush	husch-	slip away, vanish
.13	Us	aus	end, finished